I was placed on my back in pitch-black darkness...

I soon realized that I was being drawn into the shaman's state of awareness. Everything in the darkness began to feel strangely familiar while simultaneously remaining distant and foreign.

Then I saw them.

Snakes...a pit of a countless number of very large snakes, all slowly slithering and moving past each other....

The shaman touched my upper body and I was certain that he was about to put a live snake on my chest. My heart was beating rapidly now, busily pumping a full year's supply of adrenaline throughout my body in mere seconds. I was convinced that the shaman possessed the ability to read my mind and was about to confront my fear of snakes by the most direct means possible....

"In *Reality Is Just an Illusion,* Chuck Coburn takes his readers on a provocative world-wide tour in search of unorthodox wisdom. The touchstones of this voyage...are curiosity, spirituality, and humor."

—Dr. Stanley Krippner, Saybrook Institute,
Co-author, *The Mythic Path*

"This book describes the amazing personal experience which led former businessman Chuck Coburn into a full-time career as a professional psychic. Coburn recounts his odyssey in a very readable story which is both lighthearted and deeply moving."

—Robert Van de Castle, Professor Emeritus,
University of Virginia

"Humor is a wonderful teacher, and it is Chuck Coburn's ally in his appeal to develop our natural intuition and live more creative and passionate lives."

—Robert Moss, Author of *Conscious Dreaming:
A Spiritual Path for Everyday Life*

About the Author

A native Californian, Chuck Coburn received his Bachelor of Science degree from San Jose State University in 1962. For the next twenty-six years, he worked to build an $8 million construction business, receiving numerous awards including a Gold Nugget excellence award from *Builders Magazine*. In 1988, he walked away from his profitable business to devote the rest of his life to spiritual and metaphysical pursuits.

Since 1978, Chuck has served as a professional psychic, lecturer, teacher, and television host. He has worked with police agencies to locate missing persons, the FAA to pinpoint downed aircraft, and has taken part in classified parapsychology research at John F. Kennedy University in Orinda, California. His metaphysical education includes personal experiences with shamans in Brazil, Ecuador, Africa, Egypt, Hawaii, and shamans of Native American descent. He has enjoyed personal instruction and training from Gerri Patton, Dr. Stanley Krippner, Dr. Michael Harner, Kevin Ryerson, Shirley MacLaine, Angeles Arrien, John Perkins, and numerous others.

To Write to the Author

If you wish to contact the author or would like more information about this book, please write to the author in care of Llewellyn Worldwide, and we will forward your request. Both the author and publisher appreciate hearing from you. Llewellyn Worldwide cannot guarantee that every letter written to the author can be answered, but all will be forwarded. Please write to:

Chuck Coburn
c/o Llewellyn Worldwide
P.O. Box 64383, Dept. K155–4
St. Paul, MN 55164-0383, U.S.A.

Please enclose a self-addressed, stamped envelope for reply, or $1.00 to cover costs. If outside the U.S.A., enclose international postal reply coupon.

The World of Shamans, Ghosts
and Spirit Guides

Reality is just an Illusion

Chuck Coburn

1999
Llewellyn Publications
Saint Paul, Minnesota 55164-0383, U.S.A.

FIRST EDITION
First Printing, 1999

Interior design, editing and typesetting: Kjersti Monson
Cover design: Michael Matheny
Cover photo: Susan Ruggiero

Library of Congress Cataloging-in-Publication Data
Coburn, Chuck, 1939–
   Reality is just an illusion: the world of shamans, ghosts, and spirit
guides / Chuck Coburn. —1st ed.
      p.   cm.
   Includes bibliographical references (p.   ) and index.
   ISBN 1–56718–155–4
   1. Parapsychology.   I. Title.
   BF1031.C575   1999
   133–dc21   99–24438
                                             CIP

Llewellyn Publications
A Division of Llewellyn Worldwide, Ltd.
P.O. Box 64383, Dept. K155–4
St. Paul, MN 55164-0383

Printed in the United States of America

It is not uncommon to be apprehensive and fearful of new events and experiences as they suddenly challenge our otherwise complacent lives. It is this resistance to new and unfamiliar situations that often prohibits our growth.

This book is about confronting and dissipating the fear of opening to our inherent psychic abilities as we move into new levels of spirituality and metaphysical understanding.

With special thanks . . .

This book is dedicated to my good friend—let's call him Jack—as well as to all of my other friends and family members who read (and in some cases even bought) my last book—and, since then, have lobbied hard to get their names mentioned in this one . . .

. . . and to my Dad who had to leave before being able to read either.

Also by the Author

Funny You Should Say That . . .
Seed Center, 1995

Table of Contents

xi   foreword by John Perkins

xvii   introduction

1   chapter 1 / In Search
                          of the Shaman

11   chapter 2 / The Art of
                          Spiritual Healing

21   chapter 3 / Deeper Into
                          the Rain Forest

31   chapter 4 / A Bizarre
                          Healing

39   chapter 5 / Everything
                          Is Energy

51   chapter 6 / Up Close
                          and Paranormal

59   chapter 7 / A Ghost
                          in the Mirror

65   chapter 8 / **Meeting
             an Angel**

73   chapter 9 / **The Art of
             Psychic Channeling**

81   chapter 10 / **Psychic Tools
             for Divination**

91   chapter 11 / **Working with
             Spirit Guides**

101 chapter 12 / **How to Contact
             Your Guides**

111 chapter 13 / **Threatened
             by a Ghost**

119 chapter 14 / **A Haunted
             Mansion**

125 chapter 15 / **The Importance
             of Proper Closure**

133 chapter 16 / **In Search of
             Missing Persons**

139 chapter 17 / **The Search for
             Missing Objects**

149 chapter 18 / **Over the Edge
             of Perception**

159   chapter 19 / **The Psychic Community**

165   chapter 20 / **Gotta Love the Skeptics**

171   chapter 21 / **Descent to the Lower World**

181   chapter 22 / **The Anatomy of Fear**

191   chapter 23 / **How to Change the World**

199   chapter 24 / **The Impossible just Takes Longer**

207   chapter 25 / **Gettin' the Energy to Flow**

217   chapter 26 / **The Exception to the Rule**

225   chapter 27 / **Making a New Beginning**

231   bibliography

233   index

Foreword by John Perkins

Businessman and ecologist John Perkins draws extensively from three decades of experience as a consultant to the United Nations, World Bank, and Fortune 500 companies as well as his time as President and CEO of a major U.S. energy company committed to environmentally beneficial technologies. A leader in developing ways to balance business interests with ecological and social concerns, Perkins created the Pollution Offset Lease for Earth (POLE) program and has collaborated with numerous shamans to found a worldwide grass roots movement: Dream Change Coalition. He served as U.S. Representative to the U.N. Energy Commission during the 1970s. A bridge between cultures, Perkins pioneered the integration of modern and traditional transformational methods and has taught at universities on four continents. His highly acclaimed books include Shapeshifting; The World Is As You Dream It; The Stress-Free Habit; *and* Psychonavigation.

Outside the stone temple, the Andes Mountains were cloaked in darkness. Inside, a fire blazed. It warmed the chill air and the sixteen North Americans who sat in a circle around it. The shaman smiled. His ancient eyes moved slowly, taking in each of his guests. His legs were crossed and his back was against the wall.

Taita Alberto, a member of an indigenous Quechua-speaking culture that traces its traditions back to a time long before the Incas, chanted softly. Iyarina, his twenty-two-year-old daughter and a shaman in training, entered the room and sat next to him. A centuries-old tradition encourages young people to study under elder shamans of the opposite sex. She cradled her infant son in her arms.

The nine women and seven men who had journeyed from the United States included psychologists, physicians, teachers, businessmen, and a writer. They had taken this incredible journey because they wanted to learn about energy, healing, and the wisdom and rituals of the shamans who live in the mountains and rain forests of South America.

"We are entering the Fifth Pachacuti." Taita Alberto's voice was low and soft. "A magical time when the Condor and Eagle will mate."

"What is a Pachacuti?" someone asked.

"According to legends that go back long before the Spaniards, a Pachacuti is a period of time lasting about five hundred years. The legends predicted that the Fourth Pachacuti would be a time of conflict. It began at the end of the 1400s. Our forefathers prophesied that the Fifth Pachacuti, which is starting now, will be an era of union and partnership, of sharing, a time when the Condor of the South will mate with the Eagle of the North." He stood up and walked to the fire. "The Eagle is an aggressive and materialistic animal, a bird of prey; the Condor is spiritual, a good environmentalist who eats carrion. They have much to share and teach each other."

"It is why we are here," Chuck (the writer) said.

Taita Alberto's eyes held his. "It's why you are here, my brother, and why we open our doors and our hearts to you."

His words took me back to a meeting several years earlier, deep in the Amazon rain forest, with shamans from the Shuar tribe.

When I first lived with them in the late 1960s, the Shuar were noted for the ferocity of their warriors and their custom of shrinking the heads of slain enemies. By 1992, they had become very concerned about the destruction of the forests around them. When I offered my help, one of their shamans spoke the thoughts of many. "The world is as you dream it," he told me. "Your people of the

North dreamed about big factories, cars, and lots of money. Your dream came true and now you understand it is a nightmare of pollution that is destroying life as we know it. You must *change* your dream. Your people must shapeshift. We can help you. We can teach you and your people to dream Earth-honoring dreams."

The Shuar believe that the Earth is our true mother, that everything we need comes from her, and that we must sacrifice whatever is required to take care of her. The four elements are sacred. The goddess of the Earth, *Nunkui*, lives in close harmony with the goddess of the waters, *Tsunkqui,* the sun god, *Etsaa,* who brought fire, and the wind, *Nase.* Each alone is very powerful. Together, they are invincible. A fire is always kept burning in a Shuar lodge—day and night—because its energy attracts the good spirits. Rain and wind are welcomed even when they interfere with daily activities. The staple food of the Shuar, manioc root, is never harvested without first singing to Nunkui and obtaining her permission.

"You know," the Shuar shaman continued, pointing into the jungle, "the spirits are all around us. Out there in the air." He bent down and pressed his hands into the earth. "Here, Nunkui. And here." He raised his palms to the sun. "When we leave this life, we shapeshift through many stages. At last we all become the rain."

I thought about that night as I sat in the high Andes watching Iyarina prepare this group of Northerners to be healed and taught by her great grandfather. These men and women had already experienced so much. During the six days they had spent in Ecuador, they had shapeshifted. In a physical sense, they had traveled into the jungle and lived with the Shuar. They had hiked through dense jungles to the Sacred Waterfall where, according to legend, the first man and woman were created. They had taken dugout canoes down rivers that were formed in Andean glaciers and would become the mighty Amazon. Yet, their experiences had gone far beyond the physical. They had participated in all-night psychonavigational journeys led by the Shuar shaman who had spoken to me of dream change back in 1992. They had drawn upon powers and skills that previously they could not have guessed they possessed. And now here they were back in the high Andes, seated in a circle in an Incan temple, next to the highest active volcano in the world, just a few miles from the Equator. The Quechua live very differently from the Shuar; yet their ideas about the power of the dream and the need to restore balance to the Earth/human relationship are similar.

Taita Alberto performed several healings that night. He cured one U.S. psychologist of a lower back pain that had plagued her for a decade, another of migraine headaches, and a third of an intestinal disorder. He "cleansed" and energized eight more. Despite his age, he was remarkably vigorous. He was careful to constantly point out that all the healing came from Pachamama, Mother Earth; he told us that he was only a conduit who "blew nature's energy and health into others."

When the healings had been completed, most of the twelve followed Iyarina out of the shaman's lodge to watch Mama Kilya (the moon) rise from behind a gigantic volcano. A few stayed inside with me. We moved closer to the small carpet spread out on the dirt floor and asked Taita Alberto to tell us about his *huacas*—the sacred stones he had set out on the carpet before beginning the healings.

He looked his huacas over carefully. Then he took an ancient axhead into his wrinkled hands and caressed it tenderly. "This is a woman," he said. "Her name is Maria Luz. And this—" he picked up a smaller stone that was rounded like a ball with five distinctive points radiating from it (I assumed it once had a handle and served as a battle mace, possibly Incan) "is Maximo, her husband. Male and female. They must always be balanced." He raised each stone to his heart. "All of these," he said after a pause, waving his hands over a dozen beautiful stones, "are powerful spirits. They talk with me. They guide me and help bring Pachamama's healing energy into this room so I can take care of you."

He pointed toward Chuck and his wife, Shirl. "You are each powerful people who can see into the future, who know things that are revealed to few others." He held his two hands up, the palm of one facing Chuck, the other Shirl. "Male and female; it is good to have you each here and wonderful to feel your balanced power." He bowed toward them. "Welcome."

Taita Alberto picked up a bottle of *trago*—a cane sugar alcohol that is considered sacred. He took a long swig from the bottle and then, leaning forward, blew it in a fine mist across his carpet of huacas. He wiped his chin with the back of his hand. "They are happy now." He took another swig, this time swallowing it. He chuckled, his eyes sparkling in the candle light. "So am I." He passed the bottle to Chuck, encouraging him to drink, then to Shirl and the rest of us.

Later that night, after we shared food with Taita Alberto and the five younger generations of his family, we clambered onto our bus and headed for the hacienda where we would spend the night. I sat beside Chuck. Mama Kilya shone brightly through our window.

I had read Chuck's first book and knew about his psychic abilities. I had been waiting for the right moment to ask him what he could tell me about myself—now, following this evening with Taita Alberto, seemed appropriate.

He requested that we swap seats, explaining "I do my best work when you are on my left." Immediately he began to "read" me. He looked into my past and told me things about my relationships with many people, especially my parents. Then he delved into my past lives and described how my former manifestations were impacting my current one. He led me through this into the future.

It was amazing. All that he said rang true to things I either already knew or which made absolute sense to me once he said them—not just intellectually but also on a deeply emotional level. His descriptions were detailed and poetically graphic. Some of them took the form of teachings I could use to help guide me into the future. Many psychics have given me readings over the years, but none have been so inclusive or done it with such clarity.

I was very impressed. I tried to express my gratitude by telling him that I thought his powers were symbolic of the union between the Condor and the Eagle.

He turned away to look out the window, and his voice came to me almost like Taita Alberto's chanting. "The Condor of the South and the Eagle of the North." He turned back, facing me. "These are incredible times. What magic!"

I peered into his eyes. They sparkled in the moonlight. I felt certain that he was destined to share that magic with many others. "The spirit of Merlin is within you," I said. "How will you empower it?"

"I'll write another book—the next step."

Introduction

Ever imagine what it would be like to be transported to another time and place to sit at the foot of a mystic? How would you like to be able to communicate a loving thought to a family member after they've departed the physical plane, or be able to receive information from your personal angels or spirit guides about the true purpose of life—and the part you've selected to play in it?

I have . . . and through the pages of this book I will share a few of my experiences in order that you might discover *your* true purpose by activating your natural psychic self.

My bizarre metaphysical tale began twenty years ago, when I was in my mid-thirties. I was an ordinary guy, cruising through life with the statistically typical family: a wife, a son and daughter, a dog and two cats. I was a partner in a family-owned construction business and had by this time in life purchased a modest home in suburbia, accrued reasonably good moral values, and accumulated my share of credit card receipts.

Then suddenly, at 6:45 P.M. on an October Sunday evening, I discovered that I was psychic. For the next fifteen years, I experienced some truly amazing adventures and witnessed some extraordinary events.

Now, a few traditionalists might take issue with those claiming to be intuitive or psychic in *any* form. They relish quoting specific scripture to illustrate God's decree to beware of false prophets. I have no disagreement with this proclamation but, at the same time, wish to make a clear distinction between directions issued from ego-based oracles or prophets and spiritually-directed psychic or intuitive knowing.

I think most of us would agree that creativity, inspiration, and true spiritual thought originate from a source other than the organic matter in the space located between our ears. As we psychically open to input from this higher origin, we begin to understand our purpose in this life and can begin to address the unresolved karma brought forward from previous incarnations.

Shamans from around the world constantly remind us of how special it is to exist in physical form. They teach us that most of the lessons we encounter can only be learned when on *this* dimensional plane. We must complete the tasks presented, and karma earned, before we can move on to the next level of understanding. To become open to your psychic self is a means by which you can access this understanding. Being out of sync with our purpose in this life is a waste of a valuable opportunity.

My initial psychic experience nearly twenty years ago was as scary as it was dramatic. How did I suddenly know that a lady across the room—a woman I had never seen before in my life—was about to choke and would need assistance? How could I possibly explain a clear awareness of events or situations I had never previously known to even exist? I soon learned that sudden and dramatic openings are not all that unusual, particularly with those who do not believe in things metaphysical—and boy, did I fit into *that* category!

We often are more affected by fearful or unexpected experiences than the more gentle or familiar ones. Doesn't a nightmare grab your attention more than a commonplace dream? As it turned out, I was so influenced by this experience that it permanently changed my life from that of a mainstream, conservative business-oriented general contractor to a spiritually directed professional psychic.

If you receive nothing else from this book, please understand that we are *all* psychic. Haven't you experienced knowing who is on the phone when it rings . . . or sensing that something unusual is about to happen prior to its occurrence . . . or feeling that you've been somewhere before when you know you haven't?

Time Magazine, USA Today and *CNN* have reported that well over fifty percent of adults in the United States have either seen a ghost or encountered a spirit guide or angel. Over seventy-five percent think such an occurrence is possible. And yet, there are a large number of people who are reluctant to admit their psychic experiences publicly, for fear of ridicule.

My first book, *Funny You Should Say That* . . . attempted to provide the assurances we desperately seek following an abrupt psychic opening. It demonstrated how to initially contact and work with one's spirit guides or intuitive source. It related personal experiences regarding shamans, psychic surgeons, ghosts, out-of-body journeys, sacred sites and power spots, earth energies and vortexes, and other energy manifestations which can be encountered along the "yellow brick road" of what we term reality.

So—here we go again with another installment intended to take us to a *deeper* level of metaphysical comprehension. Although this book continues my personal story, it is intended to be a lighthearted approach to opening *your* psychic abilities. In addition, it may help you navigate through limiting fear and resistance as you seek to use and understand your psychic gift, opening the gateway to personal spiritual enlightenment.

Reality Is Just an Illusion covers a variety of supernatural subjects, from how to contact your angels and spirit guides to procedures for grounding yourself in physical-based reality and protecting yourself from negative energy. I've tried to provide an understanding of the many modalities of hands-on healing as well as suggest ways to tune in to your inner knowing. There is also coverage of the methodology for viewing an aura and selecting a personal sacred site. The techniques of mystic shamans, psychic channeling, creating a personal tarot deck, psychic dreaming, and the concept of God-Consciousness are all major topics in this book. Each new discussion brings us closer to the conclusion that "reality" as we know and define it is, in actuality, an illusion—an extension of our belief system. All of this information is mixed and blended with personal stories, historical perspectives, and a dash of humor for good measure.

The journey commences by taking the reader into the deep reaches of the rain forests of Ecuador and a meeting with a shaman of the Shuar head-hunting tribe. This shaman introduces us to the art of psychonavigation, non-ordinary reality, and time journeying. From there we venture to the high reaches of the Andes where we . . . ahhhh . . . but that would be telling, wouldn't it?

So settle back, take a deep breath and put the outside world on hold. What takes place on the following pages actually happened to me—a common man not unlike you or the guy next door.

No need for shots and a passport . . . enjoy the trip!

chapter 1

In Search of the Shaman

"What the heck am I doing here?" I asked myself as I sat down to journal my last several day's adventures. It was a hot and muggy afternoon, as it had been since we arrived, and I was happy to be sitting in the shade under a man-made shelter . . . such as it was. A long-legged spider on the large leaf of a tree directly in front of me had finally made her way to an unrecognizable meal, which was bound up in the heavy net of her web. As I watched, I thought about my recently consumed lunch of similar unknown origin.

For someone who tends to tentatively peek through his fingers when viewing reptiles in nature films, I had a difficult time accepting the fact that I was deep in the Amazon jungle, a six day's journey on foot to anything even vaguely resembling a town.

"The rain forests of Ecuador contain over 120 species of birds found no other place on earth," our guide had told us as we flew by chartered single-engine aircraft to a grassy clearing near this remote campsite. I hadn't dared inquire as to the number of snakes that I was convinced would be waiting for me in the flora and fauna.

Shirl, a dream worker and my wife of thirteen years, and I had signed on to a Noetic Science sponsored trip to Ecuador. This journey was an extension of our ongoing fascination with native shaman healers who were willing to share their unique and precious spiritual knowledge with ordinary people from the "outside world." This was anything but an ordinary place.

The Question is: Why Bother?

I like to think of myself as an ordinary guy—not born with a special spiritual gift, not dramatically struck with a thunderbolt of ethereal light from the heavens above. Instead, I had suddenly discovered my ability to psychically know things following a three-day personal growth workshop some twenty years ago. Prior to that, I had never considered myself to be any different from other people. Rather, I was pretty typical, having amassed a respectable amount of Boy Scout merit badges and grammar school good citizenship awards during my formative years.

Once caught up in a new way of being, however, I found that I couldn't let go. I was determined to learn everything that I could about my newly-found psychic sense. My fervent study of spirituality and metaphysics led me to discover a variety of paranormal events just waiting to be explored. I encountered enchanting ghosts in a haunted castle on the Rhine River in Germany and in a historic pub in London. I experienced an animated and informative conversation with Shirl's deceased father, who appeared in our bedroom six months after his death. I met an angel during a moment of distress and learned to communicate with my spirit guides on a daily basis. I was drawn to visit powerful and mystical sacred sites in various parts of the world, and discovered a passageway to the spirit world in my own bedroom.

What initially set me apart from others who have experienced a sudden paranormal occurrence was my obsession to *master* this natural psychic ability, which, I came to understand, awaits discovery in us all. It's a capability that eventually provides us the opportunity to explore and expand our spiritual nature as well as resolve past-life karma. My fascination with developing this psychic skill was no different than someone whose sudden middle-age intrigue with the art world motivates them to develop their creative aptitude to paint or play a musical instrument.

Psychicism is a capability we can *all* access—and through it, we just might find enlightenment.

The **Non-ordinary Nature** of **Things**

Shirl's and my search for spiritual knowledge led us to pursue new experiences and seek new teachers—our two primary purposes for this trip to Ecuador. Having been on our spiritual/psychic journey for some time, we had become increasingly aware that shamans, oracles, and mystics of numerous third world indigenous cultures were now making themselves available to those seeking to solicit their knowledge. Shirl and I felt that the understanding one could gain from this experience is essential for elevating individual spiritual awareness and assisting the planet with its healing.

The word *shaman*, originating from the Tungus tribe of Siberia, literally means "one who sees in the dark." Shamans are spiritual teachers and healers who are said to make journeys to non-ordinary reality while in an altered state of consciousness in order to remove, restore, transmute, or retrieve energy.

Shirl's fascination with shamans grew out of her exploration of alternative healing methods following the major illness of one of her children. My connection had developed through my fifteen years as a professional psychic and teacher. Together, we embarked on a spiritual worldwide quest, searching for others of like mind in Europe and Africa as well as North and South America. Our current trip to Ecuador was part of our unquenchable thirst for additional understanding regarding the metaphysical nature of things.

We were further motivated to seek this knowledge by the planetary age and time we'd both selected for our particular incarnations. Many authors have labeled the twentieth century as the so-called "new age," a greatly overused and misunderstood term and one I have increasingly grown to dislike. Many diverse cultures have surprisingly similar legends relating to this era. Some have foretold of it, referring to people at the end of this century as travelers between two worlds.

These legends speak to the anticipated expansion or quickening of planetary consciousness as we near the end of the millennium. Astrologically, it has been described as a shifting from the time of Pisces to Aquarius—from the "male" energy that began with the birth of Christ 2,000 years ago to an age of feminine and Goddess energy in which saving the planet and living in harmony with one another is the dominant ideology.

The consensus of this new age spiritual perspective suggests that our earth's human inhabitants are beginning to become aware of an energy shift—a time-warp sort of thing—wherein many are beginning to move into the next world, or four-dimensional reality. This event has been foretold by ancient civilizations such as the Hopi and Mayans as well as recognized psychics such as Edgar Cayce and Nostradamus. Our proof that these changes continue to occur is documented in numerous UFO sightings; geological changes such as earthquakes, volcanic eruptions, and weather changes; and growing interest in the plethora of new age subjects.

Still, we as a culture are often unclear on how we can personally relate to these events. Who better to assist us in this transition than the "primitive" tribal spiritual leaders or shamans, who are in greatest harmony with nature and the natural order?

Although on one level I was being driven by some unnamed force to experience all that I could, I wasn't entirely sure that I was ready to complete this spiritual transformation. At age fifty-something, I was only recently getting a handle on this "ordinary reality" stuff. I was enjoying the fruits of retirement and the good life. For me, "roughing it" had long been defined as toughing it out when the air conditioning quit in my eight-year-old Porsche.

Life was good!

"But life is an *illusion*," claim various shamans, philosophers and tribal elders from differing spiritual walks of life. What they mean is that we do not discern reality as it truly is . . . or can be.

What Is Reality?

Spiritual leaders and philosophers point out that since each of us interprets individual events differently, based on personal past physical experiences, we often assume inconsistent viewpoints, seldom agreeing on the nature of what we have encountered or observed. However, when we dream or meditate, we touch higher-dimension reality, where lack and limitation do not exist and everything is exactly how we perceive or experience it.

Take a moment to reflect on what happens when we dream. All we need to do is focus on a specific thought and it immediately becomes our experience. There are fewer rules in this less limiting consciousness. We can fly, be a larger-than-life hero, eat an unlimited amount of fattening foods, and accomplish other tasks that are equally as impossible in three-dimensional physical reality, then blend that understanding with our individual awareness.

This higher spiritual dimension is the next step up in the progression of consciousness, and the only requirement to attain it is believing that it is possible. After all, doesn't the Bible tell us: "Seek and ye shall find?" If that is not sufficient authority, how about Peter Pan, who simply tells us to *believe?*

So here I was, sitting in what our Ecuadorian guide loosely referred to as a "lodge," waiting for my wife to return from a day-hike in the jungle where she was forging rivers and climbing mountains, seeking her vision quest.

Our leader had described the physical requirements of the day's hike and it sounded a bit more dangerous than what had been presented in the brochure. The mere fact that I was in the jungle at all was evidence that I was confronting many of my basic fears, but I wasn't ready to take it *that* far. I decided to remain behind with others from our group of sixteen who had expressed similar variations on my theme.

What if I broke my leg or had a heart attack or something? How might I be able to survive, far removed from modern science and excessively expensive hospitals? Or worse, what if I was attacked by a giant anaconda? And how, in the first place, had I gotten talked into traveling on this scary venture into a foreign wilderness so many cultures removed from my own?

My vision quest had occurred several years prior when I—along with a group of equally out of shape, middle-aged male companions—spent three days alone in the California Sierra Nevada mountains. We were really "out there"—no refrigerator stocked with cold beer, no snack foods, no up-to-the-minute football scores. Following a communal sweat lodge ceremony during which we confessed our individual fears about being alone ... in the wilds ... in the dark ... we created individual campsites at a distance of at least a half-hour journey from each other.

I insisted on sleeping in a tent rather than out in the open since I was operating under the assumption that if I couldn't see the scary things I knew were out to get me, they might not be there. Although *we* were fasting, we couldn't be sure that the collective wild kingdom had agreed to the same rules. So, even though we were each on our own, we agreed to create a designated clearing where we would leave daily evidence of our survival, assuring one another that no one had been devoured by some sort of man-eating forest creature.

The challenges of the Sierra trip paled by comparison to my current location in this remote part of the rain forest. We were visiting tribes who, until recently, settled their differences by removing their opponents' heads. John Perkins, the leader of our little expedition, repeatedly assured us that they don't do that anymore . . . or at least not often. In any case, I was more focused on potential encounters with snakes than the possibility of losing a portion of my body to the locals.

John had written a book, *The World Is As You Dream It* (Destiny Books, 1994), that had caught Shirl's eye six months before. Being a self-taught dream counselor, and always seeking a new adventure, she had somehow convinced me that this was the next exotic place we should visit in our pursuit of esoteric knowledge. Since John's credentials were impressive and his shaman contacts unique, I reluctantly agreed to go along.

Planetary Consciousness 101

John Perkins was a volunteer in the Peace Corps right out of business school, and then a management consultant to the United Nations and the World Bank. He had spent most of his time in the rain forests of South America, assisting and teaching the natives the advantages of the modern mechanized world. He helped them clear the forests and build factories and power plants in order to bring the primitive culture into step with the twentieth century.

Until he woke up to what he was doing.

John realized that he was *not* helping the indigenous culture. In fact, he realized that he was actually a part of the problem. Although the Corps did much that was good, it was ultimately denying the local natives their own way of being. John felt that we were imposing our culture, our lifestyle, and our belief system on people who not only didn't understand it, but were perfectly happy with their own culture's status quo.

Journalist Joe Kane wrote a moving story about this issue (*San Francisco Examiner*, October 29, 1995). The article is about a man named Moi, an Ecuadorian native from the Amazon rain forest who traveled to Washington, D.C. to communicate the harm being inflicted on his people. He left his world of loincloth and bare feet to hand-carry a letter addressed to the "President of the United States of North America." As Mr. Kane recalled the story, Moi traveled two weeks by foot, canoe, bus, rail, and air to ask why the United States was trying to destroy his culture. "The whole world must come and see how the Heroin [tribe] live well," he wrote. "We live with the spirit of the jaguar. We do not want to be civilized by your missionaries or killed by your oil companies. Must the jaguar die so that you can have more contamination and television?"

You can imagine the official government response.

Fortunately, our planetary awareness is beginning to change. John Perkins is one of an increasing number of environmentalists beginning to touch the consciousness of the world view. Because he has devoted much of his energy to raising money to purchase the rain forest in the name of the "people," the local shamans are reciprocating in their way. They have made themselves available to teach sacred knowledge—a practice all but forgotten in the hustle and bustle of our fast-paced world.

Our trip to this isolated location, this outer edge of my Western-based comfort zone, was to seek additional understanding about this ancient knowledge, this seldom understood nature of "reality."

The World According to Shamans

So, what exactly can the shamans teach us? To begin with, let's look at their view of physical existence and how it differs from what we Westerners were taught in school. My generation was led to believe that all of reality can be defined, explained, and understood by studying the well-known laws of physics. Sir Isaac Newton said that all observable events are predictable once they are categorized and understood. He lumped all of what he termed *reality* into specific edicts such as the law of gravity, perpetual motion, and so forth.

Now, several generations later, our highly educated scientists have modified their views. My grandchildren are learning about a relatively new concept: quantum physics. Einstein and Bohr discovered that the act of observation *changes* the reality of the object or event observed. They profess that if we expect something to happen, our expectation influences the result. Modern scientists point to *quarks*, the smallest building blocks of physics, and tell us that the act of observation actually *influences* an object.

The shamans have yet another view of reality—one that hasn't changed for centuries. They believe it is not the act of observation but *how* one observes that dictates reality. They claim that we each see the reality we intend to see . . . and it is an illusion.

Who is to say that the ways of the shamans are outdated or incorrect? Doesn't our perception affect our reality? We certainly laugh more easily at someone whom we anticipate will be funny. Are we not less successful when we expect to be? Physicians are even beginning to articulate the notion that attitude has a lot to do with health. The placebo that we *expect* to cure our illness has been clinically proven to be a positive influence on recovery.

Shamans (often called seers) not only "see" things by means other than the standard five senses, but are able to *project* their intentions, effectively altering the energy of people and objects through various consciousness-changing techniques. They do not consider what they do to be a religious practice or even a belief system—it is a way of being.

Ecuadorian shamans communicate with the many aspects of nature, often singing and interacting with the plant and animal spirits of the earth. Since they depend on their environment for everything of value to them, they treat it with the respect it deserves. The Amazon Shuar people call the ground *Nunkqui,* the earth goddess.

The Andean Quechuan,[1] in the high altitudes of Ecuador and areas of Bolivia and Peru, call it *Pachamama*. Both words roughly translate to "mother earth" but, in truth, these terms encompass all of nature and the universe as a whole. These people live a simple life. They truly live in the moment. They live with an inner peace—a connection with their environment that transcends all conventional understanding.

What particularly fascinates me about these Ecuadorian rain forest shamans is that they truly live in the moment of *now*. However, when they wish to alter a present condition that arose because of past events, they simply re-dream the related events—essentially revising history with the goal of transforming the present and therefore, the future. By modifying old, outmoded belief systems, they alter the *perception* of what is to come. They believe that by re-dreaming or re-experiencing the past, the future will take on new meaning. Following this logic, they suggest that if we in the "modern world" were to change our perspective about a past emotional event, then we, too, could modify *future* perspectives and judgments about the way things are. Since these shamans believe that many diseases (dis-eases) are the result of an emotional difficulty, they contend that if you can eliminate the trauma associated with the original event, you will lessen the resultant negative physical manifestation.

One of the physical tools they use to accomplish this change and healing is *ayahuasca*, a foul-tasting hallucinatory substance derived from a local plant. It is only used ceremoniously for the purpose of enhancing spiritual growth and healing by connecting the one being healed to the spirits of the rain forest.

My party was soon to experience an ayahuasca healing. However, we would first be required to consume a significant amount of the worst-tasting, most unappetizing social beverage I've had the occasion to try, called *chincha*. Both ayahuasca and chincha are prepared using plentiful natural ingredients found in the rain forest—roots, plants . . . and human spit.

---

1. Pronounced *catch-uan.*

chapter 2

The Art of Spiritual Healing

OUR ECUADORIAN HEALER-SHAMAN from the Shuar
tribe walked barefoot through the jungle for over six
hours in order to provide ayahuasca for our little band
of travelers. Not only were we allowed to participate in the
spiritual healing ceremony, but the shaman agreed to make
a house call to our luxurious upscale Amazon lodge.

I say "upscale" because, though it was basically an eight-
room primitive structure, it was suspended off the forest
floor—suggesting only a subtle separation from all kinds
of hostile animal life much more native to this environment than us. Each six by ten foot enclosure
contained two cots complete with mattresses
and a vast assortment of very large

11

ants, spiders, and other creatures yet unnamed. To our pleasant surprise, we discovered four communal bathrooms, each with a basin, shower, and a sometimes-operational flush toilet. The good news is that there was an ample supply of water for a long shower; the bad news is that it was always ice cold!

Since I had anticipated sleeping in much less secure surroundings, I was somewhat relieved with our accommodations. I have a feeling that if there were a jungle-travelers guide book, our habitation would have been rated several stars and listed among the very best in this specific area of the sparsely populated rain forest.

Each of our five days in this part of tropical Ecuador had been filled with adventure. Webster's *Second College Edition Dictionary* defines the word *adventure* as "a daring and hazardous undertaking" or "a liking for danger." All of this was, of course, right up my wife Shirl's alley. Being more cautious than Shirl, I had always defined *adventure* as "renting a hotel room with a bathroom down the hall."

Each evening, following what was an interesting but often mysterious meal prepared in a primitive kitchen, we would generally discuss the following day's schedule of activities. This particular day we had been fasting—a necessary procedure in preparation for our long-anticipated ayahuasca ritual. At nightfall, we gathered in a central courtyard between the two wings of our lodge. It was an oval-shaped area. A large fire pit resided in the center of an open-sided enclosure under a thatched canopy roof covered with leaves and odd scraps of tin.

The **Vine** of **Death**

There was a pronounced uneasiness in the group as we neared the moment of commitment required to consume the shaman's hallucinatory potion of choice. We had been sufficiently warned of the perils of this course of action, since we would be ingesting what was said to be a poison.

By way of explanation, John Perkins told us, "The Shuar consider ayahuasca sacred. Its name literally means 'vine of death.' You are under no obligation to try it. In fact, if you ask my advice, I will discourage you. If you do decide to accept the shaman's invitation, you must understand the risks."

"Risks?" I muttered, pretending to clear my throat as eyes turned my way. Even learning to program my VCR was more appealing than what I was being asked to consider.

"The Shuar say it is their most powerful teacher," he went on. "It is dangerous, but according to them, all true learning involves taking risks." He paused, then reiterated, "This is your decision. Please remember that ayahuasca should only be consumed with the purest of intentions and an understanding of all that its name implies."

Then—as if we needed to hear more—he told us that it would cause us to become violently ill. This while we were sitting in darkness deep in the undergrowth of the third world, knowing full well that we were considered to be a meal by a large contingent of the regional reptilian species. Not exactly on my list of top ten things to do in this lifetime!

Following an animated group discussion and serious individual consideration, seven of our group of sixteen decided to take part in the ceremony. Now you have to understand, I'd never used hard or recreational drugs of any sort. My experience was limited to alcohol and an experimental puff of the funny stuff that Clinton never inhaled. I graduated from college in the very early sixties and had bypassed the loose-living hippie lifestyle—having a phony ID as a youth to buy beer for college fraternity parties was the extent of my prior lawlessness (a truth I am just now divulging to my mom).

Much to my surprise, I decided to join the minority who planned to participate.[1]

---

1. I strongly advise readers to abstain from any form of drug use. I participated in this ceremony as a person of broad experience, far along on my spiritual journey. It was presented in a healing ceremony, and administered by an authentic shaman *whose culture believes in the spiritual healing qualities of ayahuasca.* It was prepared by the shaman, who then accompanied the participants on their journeys and provided guidance.

Shirl had (of course) volunteered, along with five others—one of whom had a previous negative experience with ayahuasca but wished to try it again. Interestingly, many of those who were willing to risk the unknown peril of an arduous eight-hour trek into the rain forest earlier that day were unwilling to take this journey into the depths of the spiritual world.

We were advised to team up with a buddy who was to remain reality-grounded and was willing to experience the journey vicariously through our actions, words, and anticipated bodily purging. My partner turned out to be Lynne, a soft-spoken woman to whom I had given a psychic reading earlier in the trip and to whose conservative life philosophy I could relate. Lynne expressed a true willingness to stand by me regardless of what happened—a reassuring promise if you are depending on someone to watch over your life while you step out-of-body for awhile.

Three of the eight had committed to an additional specific healing. For some reason I still don't understand, this necessitated the shaman to spit into our individual mixtures in order that he might connect with our consciousness during the healing.

Spitting seemed to play a significant role in this culture. When one is invited into an indigenous native's home, it is customary to consume the aforementioned chincha. The drink is made the day before an expected visit by the women of the village, who chew and then spit jungle-grown manioc root into an unappetizing mixture.

Most Ecuadorian shamans also spray-spit or *camay* a powerful corn liquor called *trago* on most everything from their huacas (healing stones) to the bodies of those who come to them for healing. Camaying is a process used by healers to connect or bring unity to someone or something. It is used by Native American shamans for soul retrieval: a method used to retrieve a wandering spirit or power animal and convey the spirit back to the one being healed by blowing into the top of their head. In the case of the Ecuadorian shamans, it is done with a mouthful of liquor, but an Otavalo medicine man whom we later met in the Andes camayed fire during his ceremony.

So there we were, being informed that the unseen high priest who was lurking behind a single lit candle in the jungle darkness was busily spitting in our drinks.

This healing thing sometimes requires a real stretch of belief.

The Unbelievable Power of Belief

Having seen and experienced a number of unexplainable events during my twenty-year metaphysical search, however, this precept was not outside the realm of believability—at least not for me. Miraculous healings were something with which I had some experience.

During a trip to Brazil, I was honored with an invitation to assist Antonio De Padua, a well-known shaman, with performing some healings. Antonio asked me to help diagnose and later cleanse the energy from several of the large number of faithful who lined up daily outside his church. On the same trip, I was selected by another healer to remove a pair of ten-inch-long forceps from the back of his patient during psychic surgery in San Paulo. They had been inserted by the ghost energy of one Dr. Fritz, a surgeon who died over 100 years ago but whose spirit and knowledge many medically untrained Brazilian healers claim to channel.

I was also on the *healing* end of a bizarre ceremony wherein a Brazilian shaman wielded a scalpel inches from my abdomen, cutting into my spiritual essence—my aura. I had requested a personal healing, and the shaman both accurately diagnosed and cured my bodily disorder. The same shaman healed a bruised disk in Shirl's neck. And that's not all . . .

We once witnessed a healer emanating visible light from five of his seven chakras.[2] Truth be told, we've even spent considerable time

---

2. *Chakra* is a yoga term for wheel-shaped energy centers in the body, most often thought to be seven in number. Each chakra is believed to possess distinctive properties relating to particular body organs and deities. The lowest three (at the base of the spine, navel, and solar plexus) are said to be male, or yang, and relate to the emotions of survival, control, and power. The highest three (at the the throat, between the eyes, and at the crown of the head) are female, or yin, and relate to communication and the psychic or spiritual aspects of our nature. The heart chakra, in the center of the body, represents love—the strongest emotion in the universe. It is considered by many to be both male and female.

with healers who claim to receive their enlightenment from time-dimension travelers, or aliens from another universe.

The mere fact that someone I had never seen, miles from modern medical assistance, in the dead of night, was spitting into the poison I was soon to ingest did not seem to be a significant enough factor for me to reject the ceremony outright.

A Proverbial Flying Leap

The shaman began with the five who wished only to experience the mind-altering ceremony and not the healing. Each was presented to the shaman, who administered the sacred potion from a small bowl. This was immediately followed by a trago chaser to clear the palate. Then they were told to wait.

Before I was summoned by the shaman, my wife (who had been the first of our group to consume the ayahuasca) suddenly groaned, grabbed her tummy, and quickly exited the enclosure. It was clear where she was headed and what she was going to do. I knew she must really be sick because she'll do almost anything to avoid throwing up. When a second member of our group got violently ill, I began to reevaluate my decision.

Suddenly I heard my name being called. As I approached the shaman, I could feel his powerful presence in the darkness. He gave me the bowl and I quickly gulped the bitter drink before I could change my mind. The highly potent trago tasted sweet by comparison and I think I took several large gulps to wash the bitterness from my mouth.

By the time I returned to my partner, I could see the hallucinatory properties of the drug taking effect on those who had consumed it earlier. They seemed to be lost in their own little worlds . . . and I couldn't wait to discover mine.

I guess I expected a sudden, dramatic revelation or something because, after what seemed to be ample time, I still didn't feel anything unusual—if you didn't count the sudden need to share an impromptu and previously unrealized intellectual insight regarding the specifics of UFO technology with my partner, Lynne.

For a reason I could not explain, I possessed unexpected knowledge about a complex navigational guidance system "they" had placed under the earth's surface. I knew exact details regarding round eye-shaped beacons buried about six to ten feet deep at systemic intervals across the surface of the planet. I knew they were navigational devices, transmitting a square beam of light into space for the alien visitors to use as guidance beacons for their sojourns to our planet.

As I was beginning to pinpoint the exact locations of some of the nearby transmitters, I was summoned back to earth-bound reality by the shaman who had been preparing for the next phase of my sacred healing journey. I was led to an isolated corner of the enclosure where I prepared for what was about to happen.

I was placed on my back in pitch-black darkness. The shaman began by drinking more ayahuasca as he sang his way into an altered state—based on the amount of the toxin he must have already consumed, he should have been well on his way to complete unconsciousness. John Perkins warned me to close my eyes as the shaman began by camaying trago all over my face and exposed body. I soon realized that I was being drawn into the shaman's state of awareness. Everything in the darkness began to feel strangely familiar while simultaneously remaining distant and foreign.

Then I saw them.

Snakes . . . a pit of a countless number of very large snakes, all slowly slithering and moving past each other, not unlike the creepy scenes in an early Indiana Jones movie. And guess who was in the center of them?

While my logical mind was actively promoting the concept that this was a probably a hallucination or an illusion, a separate *feeling*-self knew that the visualization was too real to be dismissed as a simple fantasy. I shook my head numerous times in an attempt to rid myself of the images, but they promptly reappeared when I became still.

Then the shaman touched my upper body and I was certain that he was about to put a live snake on my chest. My heart was beating rapidly now, busily pumping a full year's supply of adrenaline throughout my body in mere seconds. I was convinced that the shaman possessed the ability to read my mind and was about to confront my fear of snakes by the most direct means possible.

However, I also became aware of yet a *third* self—an observer part of me that was separate from my logical and emotional bodies, calming me with a different message. This larger self was, perhaps for the first time in my life, conceptualizing that these presumably scary images might actually be . . . friendly. The detached self was introducing a subtle subtext suggesting that, although I thought I had come to heal minor physical disorders, I may actually be addressing a far larger ailment: intense fear. I remained motionless during the entire experience, afraid to move. The procedure took on a surreal form, like a dream, and I was uncertain what was real and what was imaginary.

Waking the Snake

Those who study the dream state have discovered that we are unable to move our bodies during an intense dream or nightmare due to our bodies' natural secretion of a paralyzing chemical. My ayahuasca-altered state of consciousness was definitely dream-like in that respect, having paralyzed my body even while I remained in full waking consciousness.

We were well into the healing before I realized that the snakes I was seeing were not in physical form. The shaman had just been brushing my body with a soft healing tool while shaking a rattle to accompany his continuous, consciousness-raising chanting. However, in spite of the fact that the reptiles existed only as a mental image, they were *very* real—on an experiential level.

I later realized that the snake imagery was a symbol of *kundalini*—latent spiritual energy that, when aroused, leads to enlightenment.

Kundalini is depicted on the walls of ancient temples in Egypt as a serpent that lies coiled at the base of the spine in the primary chakra, known as the *muladhara*. When it is awakened, it begins to ascend through the chakra system, unleashing powers of awareness and enlightenment as it goes.

My snake had definitely awakened.

chapter 3

Deeper into the Rain Forest

THE AYAHUASCA JOURNEY proved to be one of the most powerful experiences of my life, in spite of its dizzying and organized confusion. I got as violently sick as advertised and perceived many visual images during the eight-hour experience. I was later to learn that my experience was typical, consisting of many mental pictures appearing rapidly in one- or two-second intervals.

One of my most vivid recollections involved physically dashing outside into the jungle to upchuck what I had consumed earlier. As Lynne helped me hunt for the perfect spot, I couldn't understand why she, not having taken the drug, was stumbling around as though unable to see.

I had no difficulty in the faint light, heeding the narrow dirt footpaths leading away from the ceremonial area into the dense overgrowth.

Unearthing the Lessons

It wasn't until twenty-four hours later, when I retraced my steps from the previous evening, that I realized it had been pitch dark in the jungle that night. There was absolutely no light from the moonless midnight sky. The next day, I asked the shaman about this light phenomenon. He just smiled and nodded his head. Our translator, who had consumed ayahuasca on many prior occasions, did not need to hear his words to tell me that night vision is a common occurrence. *The spirits just make it easier for you to see,* the shaman seemed to be expressing with unspoken words from behind his full smiling face.

I also remember becoming cognizant of the many friendly eyes that appeared to be a part of all living things around me. The trees surrounding our compound, the plants of the rain forest, and even the stars in the night sky all seemed to have an awareness of us— they were watching, guiding. They were friendly and, although my partner, Lynne, had faithfully promised that she would not allow me to wander away from the safety of the enclosure, I was being drawn to the outer edge of the scary unknown. *Why are you afraid?* the eyes seemed to be asking. *Accept us . . . let go of the fear!*

Later, when my logical mind returned from its sabbatical, I realized that my perception of the eyes during an altered state suggested that everything on the planet is, in effect, conscious. Certainly, the creatures of the forest have life. One could build a convincing case that the flora and fauna interact with us as well. Scientists have been able to successfully determine, for example, that talking nicely to your houseplants produces healthier specimens than shouting at or ignoring them. Even the rocks on the ground have a consciousness— of their mass, if nothing else. The planet is indeed alive and will talk to us, if only we will listen. Mother Earth is truly vital—and the shaman's ability to speak and interact with her is his healing tool.

The day after the ceremony, we all woke up refreshed, without the hangover we fully expected after what we had done to our bodies the previous night. The shaman met with us individually and shared what he had observed while accompanying each of us on our separate experiential journeys and healings. When it was my turn, he informed me that he had removed some emotional as well as physical blocks from my body. Then he mentioned *both* the snakes and the eyes.

"How did you know that?" I stammered.

"I journeyed with you," was his simple reply.

I was dumbfounded. Even though I had become a professional psychic as result of my unexpected metaphysical awakening, I am always amazed when someone else makes an extrasensory observation. I have been doing this psychic stuff for quite awhile and I am still occasionally astonished when I issue a psychic proclamation and my clients confirm that I am correct.

"Do you know you are a healer?" the shaman added, more as a statement than a question.

This was the same question asked of me by numerous shamans and psychics whom I have encountered on my spiritual journeys throughout world, including a second healer I was soon to meet in the Ecuadorian Andes. It seemed that I was being repeatedly tutored to understand that I was not to neglect the special psychic gift I had been given—as if it had been loaned to me only on spiritual approval.

"Do not ignore what you have been given," he said. "Journey into the rain forest and talk to the spirits. Do not be afraid . . ."

Then, summoning the next of our group with a nod of his head, our brief time together was finished.

A Social Call

Following our morning reflection with the shaman, John offered to take whoever wished to join him on a physical journey into the depths of the jungle to "do lunch" with a *compadre* of Juan Gabriel Carrasco, John's affable Ecuadorian partner and our guide. Whether we were to share a meal with or were to *be* the meal for this head-hunting culture wasn't made entirely clear—but after having survived the previous evening's adventure and with the instructions of the shaman still ringing in my consciousness, I was game for just about anything.

We followed a narrow footpath made muddy by recent rain, slogging along in the knee-high wading boots we had purchased from the back of an old truck at the airport. Although it was not an easy hike, we were seemingly never out of breath, likely due to the quantity of the oxygen produced by the abundance of thick trees and plants all around us.

In addition to not being overly tired, I noticed how much more at ease I was in the thick forest, even though I was being led away from the security of our encampment hundreds of miles from anywhere, faithfully following a native guide I had met only days before. Somehow the entire environment was less fearful than it had been before consuming the ayahuasca. For some reason I had acquired a new sense of acceptance and belonging. It was as if the rain forest was observing and protecting me at the same time.

"Funny you should say that," I heard a female voice say from somewhere close behind me. I was immediately brought back to the present moment.

"That's the name of my first book," I responded, somewhat flippantly, perhaps exercising my newly found self-assurance and power.

"No—I mean funny you should have seen the eye-shaped beacon."

I turned to realize that Lynne, my sober companion from the ayahuasca journey, was speaking to me in absolute seriousness about something I had said the previous night while under the influence of the hallucinatory drug.

"I work for a rather . . . shall we say . . . *secure* section of the government and there is a fair amount of literature detailing alien eye-shaped beacons buried all over the planet," she continued. "I was interested in your description because—" She stopped abruptly, mid-sentence.

"—forget it," she finished, apparently realizing that she had said more than she should. She quickly moved several people ahead of me in the line of gringos forging the jungle path. Further attempts throughout the remainder of our trip to get her to elaborate on this subject revealed little more than a nervous smile.

As we continued walking in silence along the well-traveled but narrow, rain-soaked footpath, Juan Gabriel suddenly stopped and let out a loud hoot.

"It's the custom," he responded to our questioning looks. "It's like the jungle doorbell."

I figured we must be close to our destination, although I couldn't see any signs of a hut or village. I couldn't believe how comfortable I had become in what was previously a frightening environment. What I formerly viewed as an austere jungle had become an inviting forest—the heavy pure oxygen became an elixir and the snakes elected to be elsewhere.

I had long given up attempting to discern how Juan Gabriel knew exactly where we were, since one tree looked quite a bit like another. But I supposed he would think the same of our hectic freeways and confusing city streets.

Referring to "the jungle doorbell," he explained that men are gone for long periods of time, hunting or raiding another village. It is an accepted fact that their wives might "entertain" other men during this time, and a returning husband does not want to have to confront a tribal member in a compromising situation.

The reason this custom exists is because the life span of men in this environment is relatively short. The head-hunting wars, we were unofficially told, still take place. Therefore, anyone approaching a hut without first announcing their presence is presumed to be an antagonist and either the "approacher" or the "approachee" might end up dead.

"You know," Juan Gabriel added with a laugh, "the guy with your wife might be a good friend, so you would rather not have to deal with what you can avoid."

The group let out a collective sigh when the sound was returned, indicating that it was safe to proceed. We climbed a short hill and came upon a large oval-shaped hut that probably measured about seventy by twenty feet. It was constructed from long straight tree timbers connected by smaller sticks and covered with large leaves. From the inside, one could see the truss-shaped roof design. My construction background made me question the integrity of the arrangement—it would have not passed muster by U.S. building inspectors. However, many generations of use testified to its worthiness in this environment.

We followed Juan Gabriel and John inside, where we promptly formed a single line to individually meet our host. The Shuar warrior whose house we were in was seated with his back to the only interior wall. This wall separated the larger receiving room from the family's private quarters. His wife and children remained sequestered behind the partition as we each approached to shake his hand. He was dressed in a single cloth wrapped around his waist and he sat on a log, sharpening the tips of handmade blowgun darts.

We had been coached during our hike to this destination by Juan Gabriel about proper protocol in a native home. He cautioned us that, because this culture was quite different from our own, it was very important not to make a *faux pas*. Juan Gabriel had repeated the three most important points over and over again during the three-hour journey:

1. Avoid eye contact with tribal members of the opposite sex, because to do otherwise is to outwardly flirt . . . and we all had a fresh recollection of Juan Gabriel's story about how these people settled their disputes.

2. Remain seated. Do not venture behind the head of the household, and certainly not behind the screen where his family is sequestered. To do so would be a major insult—we shuddered to think of what might happen if we did.

3. Do not, under any circumstances, refuse to drink from the communal chincha bowl when it was presented by the warrior's wife.

The third directive, as it turned out, was the toughest assignment.

Chincha, as you know by now, is made from a bitter-tasting manioc root that, after being chewed for an extended period of time, is then spit back into a pungent-smelling, lumpy, milky-appearing substance and allowed to ferment. John assured us that it was not at all like ayahuasca and was considered a social drink.

"Chincha," he said, "is alcoholic—a sort of beer, but not a hallucinogenic." When asked about the potency, he replied, "Depends on how long it ferments—anywhere from about three to twelve percent. Whatever the proof, it'll knock your socks off!"

Having been cautioned numerous times that it would be a major insult to the host if we declined the oatmeal-thick bitter drink, we watched both Juan and John down the contents, smile, and hand the bowl back to the warrior's wife. Then it was our turn.

It was worse than you can imagine. We were offered the drink over . . . and over . . . and over. After about the fourth helping, I think it got to Shirl and she began to get somewhat giddy. She started to laugh . . . quietly at first, then her body began to shake uncontrollably as the fermented brew affected her. The woman seated next to me pointed out that the our tribal host had begun to sharpen the blowgun darts with a little more vigor as he glanced more than once in Shirl's direction. But then, fortunately for us, lunch was served. It wasn't bad once you got past the fish eyes and plantain.

Later, after getting to know the family (and receiving personal blowgun lessons) we began to appreciate the honesty, the beauty, the *simplicity* that is their lifestyle and environment. The word *stress* is not in their vocabulary. We began to comprehend firsthand the oneness of the people and their surroundings.

No clocks or schedules to make pressured demands on their lives, no unfulfilled egos to drive them to some unobtainable goal, no fear that death is the end of all existence to haunt them. They live the concept that we are truly one with all things. They illustrate an important lesson: we can gain a greater understanding of our true nature and the reality of all things by simplifying life, respecting the planet, and living in the present.

Understanding the Concept of One

The point that individual shamans from diverse cultures all over the world seem to be making is *let go and be one.*

- ◆ Let go of the pursuit of materialism. This unquenchable desire provides us merely with possessions we don't really need, and it ruins the rain forest, the environment, and the worldwide quality of life in the process.

- ◆ Let go of the ego. Once we reach "success," it is inevitably never enough; there will always be a requirement for the unobtainable *more.*

- ◆ Let go of time restraints. By creating our self-imposed schedules, pressures, and the need to do more, we are missing the primal experience of *being.*

How often do we get caught up in the drama of attempting to be someone we're not? It is almost as if we're on stage, playing a character rather than being our authentic self. Shamans are *only* themselves, often not even knowing or caring about the day of the week or the time of day. They just are.

This is not to suggest that we need to alter our lifestyle dramatically. We are conditioned to the ways of the Western world. Its many wonderful comforts and benefits are built into our way of being. It *is* to say that we should slow down. We need to stop driving ourselves in pursuit of things and goals that can never provide us with a deeper understanding of who we are.

We must begin to redirect our energy to the unseen inner experience that our ignorance and fear prevent us from discovering. We must, if we are to find our true selves. We must, if the planet is to survive. After all, this incarnation is about resolving personal as well as planetary karma—learning our spiritual lessons and returning to *One*. The dwellers of the rain forest live within the harmony of *oneness* and have let go of all restrictive fear—not an undesirable goal if you think about it.

chapter 4

A Bizarre Healing

THE REMAINDER OF our trip to Ecuador was equally fascinating and took us to the higher reaches of the Andes. We visited three shamans, each authentic and each employing slightly differing ancient energy-healing techniques in their work.

The first we were to meet was a kind, gentle, middle-aged Quechuan shaman whose appearance was not unlike the classic drawings of Jesus. He had long, flowing dark hair and deep beautiful eyes that attested to the gentleness of his soul. He walked with the ease and grace that can only come from inner spiritual calm.

He insisted that our group of sixteen stay overnight with him, sharing food prepared by his large extended family who lived scattered about the rural community. He had constructed a large circular building to house overnight visitors willing to make the long trip to his remote mountain village. He generally took no money from outsiders, but reluctantly accepted a meager sum from those whom he healed in our group.

Following a very palatable vegetarian evening meal, the shaman situated himself on one of two logs placed alongside the open fire pit in our guest lodge. With little ceremony, he began to quietly chant as one of the women from our group cautiously approached him. He motioned for her to be seated and began by gently brushing her with wild sage gathered by the children of his family. He did not inquire about her medical needs but seemed to know where to direct his attention. Although his technique consisted mainly of chanting, touching, brushing, and talking, all who experienced his healing were certain that he had accurately diagnosed their ailments.

Interestingly, his healing work took place amid seemingly distracting conversation, laughter, and activity on the part of his large family. The activity took our group by surprise, as I think we each expected the kind of reverent ceremony we knew was common to Brazilian healings. Several times during the evening, when one of his small children would approach him, he would cease what he was doing and gather the youngster lovingly in his arms. After being comforted, the child would leave and the shaman would resume his curative actions as though nothing disruptive had occurred.

The Transformation Method

There are a variety of basic healing techniques embraced by shamans worldwide, some of which I will define and discuss thoroughly in chapter 5. Many of these healing methods focus on the transformation of energy in the patient's *astral body*. The astral (or *subtle*) body is defined by A. E. Powell in his book, *The Astral Body* (Theosophical Publishing House, 1972) as:

... a vehicle, to clairvoyant sight not unlike the physical body, surrounded by an aura of flashing colours, composed of matter of an order of fineness higher than that of physical matter, in which feelings, passions, desires and emotions are expressed and which acts as a bridge or medium of transmission between the physical brain and the mind ....

The Quechuan shaman who we were visiting works by tapping into the natural forces of nature to transform the negative or disruptive energy of his client's astral body into a more positive state. He trances or channels the natural forces of fire, earth, water, and air through the ritual and rhythm of his chanting and movement. Although he offers suggestions of diet, herbs, or specific verbal affirmations, it is his channeling of the natural power of nature that measurably revitalizes the body. When the ceremony is complete and the state of mind has turned positive, the rehabilitation to good health begins.

Occasionally, the Quechuan shaman would physically *remove* the offending negative activity, discarding it to Pachamama, the earth. The earth then acts as the means of transformation, recycling the negative waste into positive and useful energy just as a plant, after being provided animal waste, restores the necessary balance that nature prefers.

Do these methods work?

One woman from our group, who had previously stated that she could not remember the last time she was without pain from her rheumatoid arthritis, began to quietly sob soon after her healing. She was pain-free. A second woman, who had partially lost her sense of smell from a bicycle accident several years prior, began to smell fragrances that she thought were lost forever.

When it was my turn, I sat before the Quechuan healer and became immersed in the peace and tranquility that he radiated. Since shamans seem to live in the continuous moment of *now*, to be in their presence is to take on a portion of their essence.

The healer began to focus his attention on my abdomen and groin—areas that have traditionally been the source of my greatest maladies. He chanted while passing his hands over my body and I could feel myself relax as if I had just ingested a drug to relieve tension and tightness. When he informed me that my karma was to work as a spiritual healer and that I was not to take my gift lightly, I knew we were connected.

He then smiled and turned to our Ecuadorian interpreter. He said something in his native tongue. I noticed that they were both regarding me with much more intensity than just a few moments before.

"What's wrong?" I questioned, not sure that I wanted to hear the answer. Juan Gabriel smiled and said that the shaman had a special cure for me, but would be unable to administer it until the following morning.

"Special cure?" I inquired cautiously, exchanging looks with Shirl who had moved in closer, and was equally concerned about the sudden change in the shaman's manner.

Juan Gabriel began to fidget and mumbled that I shouldn't worry because this is something he had seen the shaman do several times in the past. Sensing that I required more information, he again assured me that there was definitely no reason to overreact.

And then he added, "He is just going to sting you with a bee."

"No," I quickly stammered. "I am highly allergic to bee stings."

Shirl nodded her head in confirmation, having witnessed the immediate and dangerous swelling in my body that occurred the last time I was stung.

I listened carefully as Juan Gabriel translated my thoughts back to the shaman, though his sentences seemed much too short to accurately portray my mounting concern. The shaman just smiled, nodded, and muttered a few words in my direction. Then he quickly shifted his attention to the next healing.

"He will take care of it," Juan Gabriel said quietly.

Take care of it? Take care of *what*? What was he going to do? Did he fully understand my anxiety—and the potential danger? How many hundreds of miles away was the nearest hospital emergency room? Maybe I needed to sleep on the bus that I knew was parked somewhere nearby . . . I wasn't so sure that the shaman's language and cultural differences had permitted my concerns to be fully understood.

It was late by the time the shaman finally chose to terminate his healing work for the night. We all climbed into our sleeping bags around the fire pit, but the highly charged energy from the healings made it difficult for anyone to doze. Nevertheless, the next morning I awoke to a wonderfully relaxed body—and an apprehensive mind.

A Healing to Remember

We were served a light breakfast of fruits, breads, and juices prepared by families in the community. Following our meal, the shaman returned to his seat near the fire and conducted several more healings. When he finished, he got to his feet, smiled, and nodded at me. He then located Carol, a woman from our group who he had determined also required a bee sting. His eyes went back and forth between Carol and me, as though preparing us for what was to come. Then he walked away.

After a few moments, though it seemed to me like an eternity, he returned, walked directly to Carol, and raised the back of her shirt. In his cupped hand, he held a bee which he placed on her back. Seconds later, we saw Carol wince as the bee inserted his stinger.

Then the shaman turned and walked toward me. I desperately looked for Juan Gabriel, reminding him that I was *not* willing to take the risk associated with being stung by a bee. My mind was suddenly swimming with the horror stories that our family doctor had related about people suffering from allergic reactions similar to mine who had died from a single potent sting.

The issue of fear had been presented to me once again.

Within a matter of days I had been confronted with my fright of snakes, my fear of being in the jungle, and now, a potentially life-threatening bee sting. I knew spiritual pilgrimages always contained lessons, but what was I supposed to learn from this?

Did the snakes have to do with an inner fear of activating my kundalini . . . raising the quality of my own spirituality? And my fear of the vision quest, the ayahuasca, and the rain forest—were these about letting go of control? Was avoiding the potential bee sting about preconditioning myself to some sort of limitation? Was I being taught to look at things differently and to trust a new way of being?

As I watched the shaman approach, it occurred to me that in order to make the leap to higher-dimension consciousness, I must first eliminate my limitations . . . and allow a new awareness to develop.

When in Rome, do as the Romans, I thought.

Dorothy, we're not in Kansas anymore . . . .

Beyond Fear

Juan Gabriel began to speak to the shaman, who was now lifting the front of my sweatshirt and rubbing his closed hand in a circular massaging motion below my navel. As I looked into his eyes, his smile and unspoken words seemed to say *trust me.*

Then, suddenly, without warning, he plunged his fingers below my belt line! Just as quickly, he withdrew and abruptly moved on.

I was afraid to breathe.

I immediately turned to Shirl and asked in a low voice if she had seen what he had done. She admitted that whatever it was happened so quickly that she didn't know what had transpired.

"Did he have a bee in his hand?" I inquired of the woman on the other side of me as I sat motionless, uncertain of exactly what had taken place.

"Do you feel anything?" she responded. "His hand was closed so I couldn't tell if he had anything in it. You don't think he actually put a bee down your pants, do you?"

"No . . . I don't think so," I muttered more to myself than to her, feeling most comfortable in total denial. Sixteen pairs of eyes were focused on me as I sat frozen, afraid to flinch for fear of being stung.

What could he have done? I clearly had never before been in such a delicate situation.

After about five minutes (or maybe it was a day and a half—hard to tell when you're totally into the moment)—the shaman indicated that he was finished with the morning healings. I shot Juan one of those *What do I do now?!* looks and received an uncomfortable *I don't know* shrug in return.

I got up very slowly, moving as few of my body parts as necessary, and ambled toward the door as though I needed a casual breath of fresh air. I felt no movement on my abdomen but, at the same time, *knew* something was there.

Once outside, I bolted toward the outhouse—a scary experience in itself—and quickly and carefully undid my belt and eased down my jeans.

Then I heard it . . . a buzzing . . . and movement . . . in a place where one definitely does not want to hear buzzing and feel movement. As I lowered the front of my underwear, a bee that had been lodged in the elastic band of my briefs suddenly flew up, careened off my chest, and burst out the door.

I looked down to insure that all my attached body parts were in their proper place and that I hadn't been stung. I must have set the endurance record for remaining motionless in an aromatic, non-ventilated outhouse as I kept replaying in my mind what had just taken place.

How had the shaman been able to carry the bee without it stinging him? Had he somehow hypnotized it? Could it have been some kind of specially bred bee without a stinger? But don't bees die when they lose their stingers? And if *that's* true, then the big question: How did that bee know not to sting me?

Later, as we boarded our bus to leave, I asked this same question of the shaman. After a pregnant pause, his simple response was a very knowing and caring smile.

I guess Houdini never revealed his secrets either . . .

chapter 5

Everything Is Energy

WHILE IN THE Ecuadorian Andes, we were fortu-
nate to meet and receive healings from two other
shamans, one male and one female. Although they both
worked similarly, each exhibited their own modification of
time-tested techniques. Both camayed trago for the initial
cleansing as well as blew smoke on their client's body to
neutralize the negative energy as it was being removed. For
their powerful healings, both invoked the sacred spirit of
Cayambe, the tallest mountain peak in the world at zero
latitude. Finally, both had incredible success ratios.

Now, in order to even begin to comprehend how their unusual (to say the least)
actions can heal the human body,

one must first expand one's basic understanding of how shaman-led cultures view reality.

Many indigenous peoples throughout the world believe that *everything* is living energy and is interconnected with everything else. All of creation is filled with spiritual essence, from human beings to the lowest forms of plant life and minerals. Nothing is really separate or "owned" by anyone, but is for the use of all.

Shamans observe the natural cycle of the seasons and how nature continually attempts to return the balance the Creator originally intended. They will tell you that all things are from the earth and eventually will return to the earth. One's waste is another's food. They believe that even discarded negative energy can be recycled.

Shamans believe that all things work more effectively when in harmony and balance with everything else. Since they understand that everything has purpose and a spiritual cause, they contend that sickness only occurs when we are out of balance with the natural forces of nature.

The shaman's approach to treating this dis-eased state, then, is to eliminate or alter the initial cause of disharmony. So how do they determine that disharmony exists? Some shamans perceive the malady by clairvoyant means—they see it in their psychic mind's eye. It might take the form of a recognizable physical entity that is familiar to their culture such as a dangerous animal, sharp thorn, or other non-harmonious vision. Other shamans might discern the problem clairaudiently, perhaps by listening to the spirits of the forest or the whispering wind. Still others feel it by tuning their bodies in to the vibration of the one seeking to be healed. Each shaman has his or her own method of dealing with this intrusive sickness, and each has his or her own dramatic style.

The Five Methods of Spiritual Healing

We've already discussed the power of belief. Not surprisingly, an essential ingredient in any healing is the recipient's belief in the process. Whether you are undergoing treatment from a leading physician in a state-of-the-art medical facility in the States or receiving revitalized energy from a shaman with a headdress and a rattle, faith in the process is necessary in order to receive the maximum benefit. The mind plays a critical role in healings, regardless of the source of the treatment.

Shirl and I have encountered a number of healing techniques worldwide, including extraction; transmutation; soul retrieval; depossession; and the summoning of power animals, spirit guides, or natural energy forces to provide the healing. Prayer and meditation are also proven healing aids.

Extraction

The extraction method removes disharmony by employing some means of psychic surgery. When in Brazil, we observed a shaman physically insert his hand, or an instrument, into the patient's body to remove or alter the offending energy. On the same trip, we witnessed a South American mystic cut into the spiritual (rather than physical) body with a surgeon's sharp scalpel. One even removed the negative energy by sucking it into his mouth and discarding it, carefully insuring that it did not enter his own body in the process.

Included in this category are those who extract the obstacles blocking the natural flow of bodily energy from an altered state of consciousness, such as the Ecuadorian rain forest shaman you have already met. He used ayahuasca to provide a means by which to locate the blockage and remove it, all the while being assisted by the native spiritual healing forces around him.

Shirl and I have been trained regarding the placement of our hands on a patient in order to spiritually extract the image that we "see" as being disruptive. The offending energy is then returned to the earth or discarded into water. It will eventually transform back to the balance and harmony that nature demands.

Transmutation

The second technique is the transmutation of negative energy, which we have personally observed in both Africa and South America. It is a process wherein the shaman transmutes, or alters, the energy without removing it. To accomplish this, he aligns himself with one of the positive forces of nature and then merges his energy with that of his patient. The result is the transformation of energy into a positive force. Some introduce an additional energy to complete the change, as a Western-trained physician might do when prescribing a supporting elixir or drug.

Soul Retrieval

The third method, soul retrieval, is performed when a portion of the client's consciousness is discovered to have left their body as a result of an emotional trauma such as rape, neglect, or shock. Illness or possession is often the consequence of an external energy finding a home in the space vacated by a wandering or powerless soul. Returning war veterans have often been emotionally marred by their experiences and can be said to fit into this category.

Shamans believe that the cause of such a client's disease is the loss of their soul or personal power. They will often spiritually shapeshift into a bird or other animal to retrieve what the patient has lost.

Depossession

A fourth means of healing is by way of depossession, or obsession. It is a process shamans employ in order to remove an external force such as a wandering ghost or evil spirit that has attached itself to a physical body. Brazilian shamans often begin by journeying from the middle world to the non-ordinary reality of the upper or lower worlds in order to diagnose the problem. The shaman then removes the obtrusive energy, often discarding it or thrusting it into the body of one of their spiritual priests who would then overpower it and discharge the residual into another dimension.

A curse, negative thought, or inappropriate action directed against an individual or nature has been thought to cause this manner of discord as well. I am reminded of a situation in which a woman in California became so angry and upset about her boyfriend terminating their relationship that she effectively placed a curse on him. A Shaman subsequently found this curse to be the cause of a major illness experienced by the boyfriend's future wife. The shaman removed the curse and the wife quickly recovered.

The Shuar shamans of Ecuador call negative thoughts "magical darts" and consciously attempt to avoid such destructive thoughts, believing that whatever is sent out will come back.

Power Animals and Spirit Guides

The fifth method is working with or through a personal power animal or spirit guide. Shamans employing this method work from an altered state of consciousness in which they journey either to the upper spiritual world to work with the Creative Force, guides, or angels or to the lower world to meet with or empower the patient's power animal to bring about the necessary cure. A few shamans cure aliments by calling on the natural forces of nature while remaining present in the middle world.

The **Western Healer**

Common to all of the shamanistic methods of healing is the healer's ability to access other states of consciousness at will. Having visited and returned from the world of the dead on many occasions, it is said that a shaman dies only when he chooses to let go of his power.

An obvious illustration of how Western cultures differ in their approach to healing is the approach used by modern physicians in the United States, who tend to diagnose and treat the bodily symptoms rather than the *initial cause* of the malady. These doctors will prescribe a drug to mask pain or cut into the body to remove a dysfunctional organ. Shamans, on the other hand, work to recreate the form that nature intended. These native spiritualists have mastered the necessary techniques to convert negative or out-of-balance energy into positive life force. They often place themselves in concert with natural earth energy and connect it to the unity of all things. Said another way, they merge with the energy of the plants, animals, rivers, rocks, fire, or water that they find sacred and then channel the harmony found therein.

Now, this is not to discount the value of Western-based modern medical science. In fact, medical viewpoints are beginning to change. More and more medical schools are adding courses on holistic and alternative medicine, suggesting that alternative methods of healing are extremely successful in cultures that are willing to fully accept them. In fact, if you were to visit the most modern hospital in Brasilia, the ultramodern capital city of Brazil, you would find that the medical staff is composed of a mixture of modern physicians in white coats alongside shamans dressed in ceremonial garb.

Prayer

It is a well-documented fact that a placebo provided by a trusted physician often initiates or aids healing. It has also been statistically documented by researchers that religious patients who pray prior to surgery have a better chance of survival than those who do not. A 1975 study at Dartmouth suggested that those who drew comfort from prayer had a three times better chance of surviving a heart attack than those who were not religious.

Supporting this claim, *Time Magazine* (June 24, 1996) reported that a *Time/CNN* poll found that eighty-two percent of Americans surveyed believed in the healing power of personal prayer. The same magazine reported that Dr. Randolph Byrd completed a study about prayer at San Francisco General Hospital. Over a period of time, he invited born-again Christians to pray for half of the nearly 400 coronary-care patients at his hospital. He discovered that the half who had *not* been prayed for were "five times more likely to need antibiotics and three times as likely to develop complications" as those who were the recipients of prayer.

Meditation

Meditation, like prayer, has been found to be helpful. Herbert Benson wrote a best-selling book, *The Relaxation Response* (Morrow, 1975), in which he reported that patients can diminish a number of stress-related illnesses by practicing a simple form of meditation. In fact, he found that "seventy-five percent of insomniacs began to sleep normally, thirty-five percent of infertile women became pregnant and thirty-four percent of chronic-pain sufferers reduced their use of painkilling drugs."

The Skeptic Within

Assuming that we can accept prayer and meditation as potential healing aids, why does our society as a whole question the value of two hallmarks of the shaman—faith and belief? Granted, to trust your well-being to an Ecuadorian healer rubbing an ordinary chicken egg on your body is a stretch of faith. But to discount the power of *any* method of natural healing by indigenous shamans out of ignorance or prejudice only narrows one's available options for healing.

Our Journey Continues

The woman shaman we encountered in Ecuador heals by removing negative, non-desirable energy and releasing it to nature. The day we were there, she rubbed eggs vigorously on each of the bodies she was treating before breaking the eggs and spilling the blackened yokes into Pachamama. She finished by camaying freshly ground cinnamon with trago, then providing a liquid elixir of rose petals and trago for her patient's consumption as well as a talisman of three red carnations to be worn around the neck until they fell off.

Maybe it was more than just her crown of feathers, the white ceremonial garment and the chanting while in an altered state that distinguished her from the stereotypical Western-trained medical school graduate . . . .

The male shaman we visited in the Andes lived on a nearby plateau located in the center of three powerful mountains. Our bus, often required to travel off-road and traverse open fields, arrived at his home late one afternoon. Planning the exact route was difficult because John and Juan Gabriel never knew which of the shamans would be available until we arrived at our destination. Telephones and fax machines were not a staple of Andean rural culture. Healing was done when needed, not by appointment.

Still, whenever we arrived at a shaman's house, they somehow knew we were en route. Maybe they were tipped off by the herds of llamas, goats, and cattle we encountered along the way.

When we reached our destination, the mountain shaman was waiting, as though he had anticipated our arrival. John instructed our group to enter the shaman's "house" while he completed the arrangements for our visit. There was no mistaking the entry to the abode, since cattle and goats were freely going in and out.

We were ushered into a completely enclosed courtyard, which appeared to be the primary habitat of the shaman's animals. It reminded Shirl and me of the dwellings of African indigenous shamans, who also allow their herds free rein in their living quarters. Since the cattle are among their most important possessions, it was natural that they would occupy living space alongside family members. Carefully watching where we stepped, we were ushered into an interior room set aside for healing work. It was apparent that it doubled as a stable . . . .

During all of our metaphysical experiences in Ecuador, members of shamans' families were involved in the healing process. The mystic who we encountered in the rain forest had been assisted by his wife—she had accompanied him on his long journey through the forest. The healer with the beautiful eyes had gathered his entire family to provide safe and familiar energy while he worked. The woman shaman had been assisted by her thirteen-year-old granddaughter, who had begun her apprenticeship many years before. The Ecuadorian shaman in whose house we now stood must have put out the telepathic call for assistance because his wife and several of his brothers and children suddenly appeared, having traveled some distance to get there.

Four of us had volunteered to experience what the healer had to offer. John only smiled when questioned as to what specific technique would be practiced.

Unlike the others, this shaman worked with two of our group at the same time. Another difference was that he verbally diagnosed the state of the health of each person standing before him. At the same time, he alternated camaying the trago and consuming it. The remaining family members each had their own task, such as lighting candles, laying out the shaman's paraphernalia, blowing smoke, and camaying everything that moved.

Also unlike the other shamans, he picked up a candle. He took a large swig of the now almost empty bottle and promptly camayed the alcoholic trago through the flame of the candle, igniting the liquid into a ball of fire. This envelope of flame cascaded over the patient's body, momentarily engulfing him or her in a flash of heat.

"I heal with fire," he said, as if we needed an explanation.

Each time he camayed a flame those being healed would momentarily pull back and then lean forward again as if reaching out for some unseen residual energy. The shaman repeated this process maybe three or four times on each person. Then his assistants began sucking out the isolated negative energy, regurgitating it onto the dirt floor in the rear of the room.

When the evening activities had concluded, Shirl and I could observe the eerie, psychic luminescence as if it had left an imprint on the whitewashed walls. Everyone who had witnessed the procedure sensed the spiritual afterglow, which remained in the room long after the healings had been completed.

Fire, of course, is about transformation.[1] Native Americans traditionally used the smoke and fire of a ceremonial peace pipe to release truth and seal agreements. They utilized smoke and fire from the sweat lodge to transform old ways into new commitments. The fire of cremation following a death is thought to release or transform the soul from the physical world to the spiritual. The yogi purifies the chakra wheels of energy by the ceremonial use of fire. The healing shaman of Ecuador transforms the aura or energy body of his patients much as we might change the temperature of the room by heating the air.

"It didn't really hurt," one receiving the fire healing reported later. "I feel very much at peace." Although clearly hesitant prior to the ceremony, his face more clearly radiated what his words were attempting to express.

I don't think this particular technique is part of the AMA lexicon.

Unfortunately, we missed seeing the "guinea pig shaman" who, we were told, diagnosed illnesses by ceremoniously rubbing a live pig over the patient's body. If it is a life-threatening disease, the pig is

---

1. If you want to get rid of something that doesn't work in your life—an outmoded way of being . . . a fear . . . a limitation—write down what you want to change on a piece of paper and place it in a ceremonial fire, knowing that its hold on you is being released as the paper burns and turns into ash. Then scatter the ashes to the four winds. This is the first stage of a powerful process of transformation.

said to assume the ailments of the person being treated and, sadly, the animal often dies in the process. The pig is then dissected so that the shaman can authenticate his diagnosis.

Other shamans heal with medicinal plants and flower essences buried in the earth. One shaman instructs visitors to plant a young cactus near the site of the healing and psychonavigate[2] back to it from time to time for purposes of clarity and inspiration.

Evaluating the Results

Determining which shaman was the "best" healer depended on which one each of us had experienced. Every one of us had at least one healing and some had more. In retrospect, we each somehow intuitively knew which healer to choose in spite of the fact that we had no advance knowledge of their individual techniques. Everyone who was healed, whether they had a specific symptom or not, was definitely changed by the experience.

The shaman with the "Jesus eyes" was the best healer for me. He touched the core of my being. Just to have been in his presence was a spiritual experience. I have yet to determine the long-term effects of my healing with the bee, but the physical discomforts I was experiencing up to that point dissipated almost immediately after the ceremony.

If you were to ask Shirl's opinion, she might report that she was most emotionally moved by the woman who realigned her energy by rubbing her body with an egg, opening her to a heightened sense of being. That is, assuming you discount Shirl's dramatic encounter with a hallucinatory image from her ayahuasca journey shortly after we arrived back home . . . .

---

2. John Perkins defines *psychonavigation* as an Ecuadorian shaman method of navigating or visiting a physical destination or a source of inner wisdom by means of psychic visions or dream wanderings to acquire knowledge or insight.

chapter 6

Up Close and Paranormal

WE RETURNED HOME to the plethora of unopened mail and unanswered phone calls one might expect after a lengthy trip, and attempted to settle into our normal routine as quickly as possible. I immediately became immersed in radio interviews and promotional efforts for my first book. Shirl directed her attention to her dream work and grandchildren.

About a week after acclimating to the hectic lifestyle that we constantly pledge to simplify but never do, we decided to attend a meeting of a metaphysical organization to which we belong. I had happened upon their monthly mailing hiding at the bottom of my in-basket and noticed that the evening's program was, synchronistically, about ghosts and shamanism. When I read that the speaker was a well-known authority and that we could meet him at a local restaurant prior to his presentation, we knew we had to go.

Shortly after we arrived at the restaurant, we were informed that the entire program had been canceled due to a last-minute illness. Because a group of us had gathered to meet him, we decided to stay for dinner and discuss the subject matter with others of like mind. Not having previously met, we each introduced ourselves in turn and briefly spoke of our interest in the subject of the evening's scheduled lecture.

Dee, a woman sitting next to Shirl, identified herself as a hypnotherapist whose principal focus was to assist people suffering the loss of a loved one. Dee said she had come to realize that the generally accepted therapy methods she had learned in school were somewhat limited. She reported that she had studied other cultures, searching for more successful methods to bring her clients' mourning to completion. She had recently discovered a somewhat unusual method with which she had been having remarkable success.

With further prompting, she disclosed that because she had always believed that contact with the departed on some conscious level was possible, she had constructed a darkened booth in her home and had been able to successfully connect the bereaved with the deceased.

There was dead silence (so to speak).

Someone across the table spoke up, quoting statistics suggesting that more than half the adults in the United States have claimed to have had an experience with a ghost or angel. The man next to me said he was certain that the creepy feelings and unexplainable sounds he heard late at night indicated his proximity to a supernatural opening in an area of his house. Someone else listed the large number of books, popular movies, and television programs which have exploited such ghostly themes, indicating that many others must have similar feelings. When it was our turn, Shirl and I shared that our interest in this subject began when Shirl's father had contacted us—six months after his death!

Needless to say, we all stayed far into the night until the owner insisted on closing the restaurant. During the course of the evening we discussed the subject in depth, each from a different perspective.

A Brief History of Ghostly Relations

During our discussion, the group quickly agreed that contacting spirits, or *spiritualism*, was not a new phenomenon. We learned that it first became popular in Europe in the 1850s when séances and table-rapping were openly demonstrated by two sisters, Maggie and Kate Fox. This concept became so accepted that such people as Queen Victoria, Prince Albert, Napoleon III, Czar Alexander II, and even Abraham Lincoln reportedly took direction from the spirits who were manifested by this process. Harriet Beecher Stowe's *Uncle Tom's Cabin*—the novel that helped trigger the Civil War—was said to have been written with the guidance of spirits. Thomas Edison reportedly devised the phonograph in an attempt to record them.

Of course, even a century or two ago summoning spirits was nothing novel—shamans had been doing it for ages!

Cultures all over the world have not only believed that it was *possible* to contact deceased energies, but have often sought ways to *avoid* them. For example, it was traditional in the ancient West Indies' culture for a widow to wear red underwear to keep the spirit of the deceased husband away after his death. Siberian residents would purposely take a confusing route home from the funeral in order to prevent the deceased spirit from following them. Early residents in Fiji attempted to disguise the door to their abode following a funeral so the departed spirit of the family member could not enter. Australian aborigines used to go so far as to tie the hands and feet of the dead to restrict them. In Bali they would actually twirl the corpse before burying it in order to disorient the spirit and prevent its return.

The September 6, 1996 issue of *Time* magazine reported on a five-century old Dogon Dama burial ceremony in Mali, Africa. This culture is so fixated on preventing dead spirits from returning from the afterworld that their funeral ceremonies last six weeks and only take place every *twelve years!* They believe that to enter the burial cave during the intervening period of time would unleash the deceased spirits upon the village.

Our own culture is impacted by similar beliefs. For instance, do you know why we traditionally wear black at funerals? It's a throwback to the old belief that black makes the living invisible to ghosts.

Making Contact

I actually experienced a form of spiritual viewing early in my psychic development stage as I began to learn how to communicate with my spirit guides or angels. I had been given an exercise by a group that I met with at that time—it was to sit in a darkened space and, for a long period of time, gaze with "soft eyes" into a mirror until I could perceive my face change, often for just a split second. It was suggested that I would be able to glimpse a past life . . . an aspect of myself from which I had matured. I found some success with this, as did others in my group. Still, for lack of a better scientific explanation, I largely discounted the process at that time as an illusion or trick of the eyes.

As the evening progressed, Shirl became particularly intrigued with Dee's story and the room she had constructed in her house to access the spiritual world. Shirl had always wanted to be able to contact her grandfather who had died shortly before she was born. They were born on the same day—Halloween—and she had collected old photos of him throughout the years, seeking details from family members who might be able to elaborate on his life. To share the same birthday with him had created a special bond between them, even though they had never met. Might this be her chance?

Day of the Dead

Halloween, of course, is a day associated with ghostly activity. Centuries ago Europeans knew Halloween as "All Hallows E'en." It was a serious and respected holiday observed on the evening preceding All Hallows or All Saints Day on November 1. They traced the Halloween tradition as far back as the Celtic festival of Samhain, which heralded the Celtic new year. Because this day marked the start of winter's cold and darkness and was the midpoint between the autumn equinox and winter solstice, it eventually became associated with death. This was the time when spirits were thought to be able to slip through the seam of adjoining worlds, free to roam the earth. Latin Americans have a similar celebration on November 2, just one day later. They call their holiday *Dia de los Muertos* (Day of the Dead).

By the Middle Ages, this day had become associated with witches and sorcerers, as had many of the misunderstood mystical traditions. Fire festivals were held in many medieval cities on Halloween during which great towers were built and a maid and young boy were placed on the top to be consumed in the ensuing fire. To this day, Santa Fe, New Mexico holds a symbolic fire festival, although few probably know the origin of their celebration. The modern tradition of trick-or-treating actually developed from the belief that to rid yourself of these deceased wandering souls, you fed them before leading them out of town. Even the Halloween mask we wear is a means to hide (or mask) the spirit self as we "become" the animal or lower self through the our chosen costume.

Halloween is also the fortieth day following the autumn equinox. Those who are into numerology consider forty to be a special number. In the Bible, the mystical number forty repeatedly appears— Christ's forty days in the wilderness, the forty years of Jewish bondage, the forty days that Moses spent on Mt. Sinai, and the forty days of rain during the flood are all examples.

Forty is also the equivalent of four times ten, which are important numbers in their own right. Four represents the four corners of the earth in the lore of many cultures as well as the number of seasons and the number of levels of consciousness (physical, emotional, mental and spirit). These are just the most obvious examples. Ten is the number of accomplishment—the number on which the decimal system is based, the number of God's commandments, and so on. Halloween is the eve of All Saints Day, and All Saints Day is the forty-first day—when the good or surviving souls are believed to become saints.

Considering all of the above, it's easy to see that Halloween is a special day . . . a day when the living and the dead are in closer proximity than many of us find comfortable.

Pai Ely Delivers an Unexpected Message

Shirl's Halloween-born grandfather had been on her mind often due to a number of synchronistic events that brought his name or image to her attention. It was almost as if he had been attempting to reach out and connect with her. Now, late in October, just days away from the celebration of their common date of birth, he was in her thoughts again—and a dramatic event in our home was about to bring him to the forefront of Shirl's consciousness.

The incident involved Pai Ely, an incredibly powerful shaman we had met and befriended on a metaphysical trip with the Institute of Noetic Sciences to Brazil. After we had learned that he would be a featured participant at an alternative healing conference in California, we invited him to a gathering at our house. Much to our joy and surprise, he accepted our request and agreed to share his views on shamanistic healing with a few select friends.

At his instruction, all those who attended wore only white clothing. Brazilian healers, as well as others throughout the world, often request that all those who assist, observe, and participate in healing ceremonies wear only white. Pai Ely was well-received by the group. He shared some of his knowledge and performed energy transformations and healings, including an unexpected psychic surgery on me.

When I was in Brazil a few years before, I sought a healing from him for my colitis. He recalled our time together, including the specific details of our session, and asked if he could perform a follow-up surgery.

I wondered if my insurance agent had an appropriate check-box with which to deny *this* claim . . . .

Pai Ely had me lay down on the floor about ten feet from where he was seated. He entered easily into a trance and summoned the energy of a South American doctor to do the healing work. This particular procedure seemed somewhat unusual to our guests for several reasons: First, we were in North America and that was one heck of a house call. Second, the doctor had been dead for about 100 years.

Although calling in a deceased healing spirit was a common occurrence with other Brazilian shamans, I was surprised that Pai Ely was using this procedure. It had not previously been his style. His common method of healing had been to remove negative energy by summoning nature spirits for assistance while violently shaking his patient's arms and hands to release the unwanted energy. Shirl and I had witnessed this procedure numerous times and we had personally experienced a healing for Shirl's daughter through our presence in a ceremony.

As he began his work, he spoke aloud in Portuguese. Before I received the English translation, I was aware of a light burning sensation in my lower abdomen. It was as if someone was moving a blunt object down my stomach. To insure no one was playing a trick on me, I opened my eyes and peeked.

"The surgeon has just made an incision," the interpreter translated. Then I felt something moving in my lower abdomen or intestines, as if I was being gently massaged from inside my body. It was soothing and I experienced a need to relax into the feeling.

"Relax," translated the interpreter as though reading my thoughts. After a short while, the sensation ceased. I felt like someone had retraced the line drawn on my body earlier—this time from the bottom up.

"I am closing the incision," came the English interpretation.

It was done. I sat up slowly, not wanting to rip my spiritual stitches. Pai Ely reported that all was okay but that his original healing was progressing more slowly than he had hoped. I confirmed that the majority of my symptoms had ceased following his work in Brazil and I had sensed that the colitis had been minimized or was at least dormant. Pai Ely sighed, then added that other shamanic healers would be assisting me to release additional emotional blocks to aid in this healing. At the time, our trip to Ecuador had yet to be planned!

While he was in our home, we invited Pai Ely into the room where Shirl and I do our psychic and dream work. He instantly loved the energy of the room and enthusiastically set about performing a brief cleansing and purification ceremony.

When he completed the ritual, he glanced at the ceiling and casually asked me if I knew the energy he saw lingering about. I told him that it was probably one of my spirit guides. I described the "physical" appearance of Sami, but Pai Ely shook his head in disagreement.

I then mentioned the Native American-appearing ghost form that used to regularly enter our house through an energy vortex we have since closed by way of a feng shui ceremony. "He still seems to drop in on us occasionally, as would a long lost friend," I added.

He shook his head from side to side a second time. "There is an energy in here—it's a man who wants to make a connection with one of you."

"Who is it?" I questioned.

He closed his eyes tight, then opened them and looked at Shirl.

"It's your grandfather on your mother's side!" His description of the man eerily corresponded to an image of Shirl's grandfather in an old family photograph.

"He loves you very much and feels left out of your life . . . he wants to be a part of it now." Pai Ely said haltingly.

Then he took one last look around the room and headed for the door. "Oh, by the way—" he added with a backward glance, "It was him who asked me to perform the surgery."

Little did Shirl know that she would soon have the chance to meet her grandfather one on one . . . .

chapter 7

A **Ghost** in the **Mirror**

SHIRL CALLED DEE, the woman hypnotherapist,
on the day following our meeting in the restaurant.
While scheduling an appointment, Shirl made it clear
that she did not desire a full-on therapy session. Instead,
she simply wished to sit in Dee's black box and attempt to
connect with her grandfather at a time that was on or
near the date of their common birth.

"Manteum," Dee responded.

"Excuse me?"

"Manteum," the therapist repeated. "The black box
isn't a box. It's a small room or interdimensional
chamber as popularized by Raymond Moody
in his book, *Reunions*."[1]

Dee clarified that the word *manteum* was from the Latin word *psychomanteum*, which means "seat of the seer." It was simply an enclosure where the living might encounter those who are no longer on the physical plane. She went on to explain that the Greeks had a similar word, *necromantis*, which roughly translates to "divination from the dead." Necromantis is a word that was first used by oracles, the most well known being the Oracle of Delphi—a Greek woman whose psychic visions were sought by kings and generals from the far corners of the world prior to committing themselves to major decisions that would ultimately affect world history.[2]

I knew that this concept was not limited to the Greeks or even ancient Europeans. Numerous cultures, although having developed continents apart and out of contact with one another, share uncannily common spiritual beliefs. Many traditional societies, such as the ancient Hawaiians and Egyptians, believed that we have an inner doorway—for most of us, it stays closed and functions as something of a mirror, reflecting our stuff back to us. But for some people (properly prepared during secret initiation ceremonies), the doorway opens and reveals glimpses of the spirit world, the past, or even the future.

Dr. Hank Wesselman, in his book *Spiritwalker: Messages from the Future* (Bantam Books, 1995), describes what he claims to be his shamanic dreamtime journeys to a future 5,000 years from now. He writes that, when these connections are activated through mental processes and then charged with emotion and feeling, it becomes possible to send and receive thoughts and even images if you know how to do it.

"So," Dee finished, "let's see when we can schedule you." After a brief pause, she came back to the phone, her voice expressing excitement.

"Oh my gosh, what synchronicity! Would you believe the first open date I have is on Halloween? That sounds appropriate, don't you think?"

---

1. Moody, Raymond and Paul Perry. *Reunions: Visionary Encounters with Departed Loved Ones.* New York: Villard Books, 1993.

2. A number of women held the title "Oracle of Delphi," but there was only a single resident oracle at any given time.

"Funny you should say that," was Shirl's quick reply. She then requested directions to Dee's home.

The **Manteum**

It has been a tradition around our house that on Halloween night Shirl dresses up as a witch for the trick-or-treaters. But now that she is a grandmother, she begins the fun earlier in the day, volunteering to be a show-and-tell item for her grandchildren. She visits their classrooms in her witch's apparel and shares Halloween folklore, tells stories, plays games, and passes out treats.

In fact, when the older neighborhood kids come to our house on Halloween, they know they have to sing "Happy Birthday" before they receive their rewards. This practice often confuses the little ones, who have not yet been properly programmed to sing the birthday song at the same time they are struggling to understand the concept of trick-or-treating.

Because the classroom activities took longer than expected, it turned out that Shirl went to her appointment with Dee directly from the school. Having no time to go home and change, she was still dressed as a witch. *How appropriate*, she thought as she drove to the therapist's house. On Halloween, she would be sitting in a darkened room dressed as a witch, intending to speak to her dead grandfather whom she had never met and whose birthday she shared.

Dee greeted Shirl at the door and showed her to the room that Dee had set aside for her work. She had partitioned half of a spare bedroom with a black curtain and covered the remaining interior walls of this cubicle with jet black drapes. On one wall she had hung a mirror in an ornate black frame.

Dee requested that before beginning the process, they first sit and talk. She told Shirl that before she entered the manteum, she was to focus on whomever she wished to contact in order to bring greater clarity to the experience. Dee reminded Shirl to leave her expectations at the door and to be open to whatever happened . . . or didn't happen. Finally, Shirl walked into the manteum and sat down on the chair, which had been placed facing the mirror.

"I will return in forty-five minutes, but feel free to leave earlier if you wish—or you may stay longer if necessary," Dee instructed. "If you see or feel anything, just let it happen," Dee reiterated as she drew the curtain behind her and departed the room.

Her heart pounding with excitement, Shirl acclimated her eyes to the dim light and overwhelming sound of silence. The mirror had been placed in such a way as to ensure that she could not see her own reflection—only the dark drapes on the wall above and behind her.

She had purposely removed her wrist watch so that time would not be a factor. Both of us have come to learn that time is a maneuvering or limiting force in our culture—we've all been socialized to adapt our expectations to a specific time frame. *Shouldn't I be feeling something by now?* or *Isn't it time we were finished?* are questions our society interjects unnecessarily onto reality. Shirl and I look at it like this:

- Let go of time and you minimize your limitations.

- Minimize your limitations and you have come closer to discovering your truth.

- Discover your truth and you are on your way to experiencing your true reality.

Her mind wandered as it briefly replayed her day's activities. She glanced down at her witch's outfit and thought of the irony of the situation. "Grandpa, I'm dressed up for our birthday," she found herself saying. "They burned women at the stake centuries ago for less than what I'm doing now . . ."

Then—she saw it!

The mirror . . . the drapes . . . . These were the *very same images* that had appeared over and over while Shirl was on her night-long ayahuasca journey in the rain forest of Ecuador. During the height of her visionary experience, she had repeatedly seen a mirror and frame exactly like the one now directly in front of her. She remembered, in the reflection of the mirror during her ayahuasca journey, black drapery with folds and creases identical to what she was now observing months later in the manteum. It occurred to her that it looked like . . . a *doorway*.

As she focused on this new discovery, she began to be aware of faint images of ectoplasm floating around—and colors . . . red . . . green. She felt her body tingle as if it were on the receiving end of a slight electrical charge or static electricity. This detail is interesting, indeed, since psychic researchers theorize that electrical charges are associated with metaphysical occurrences. I am convinced that the shock I received as a child (I inserted a hairpin into an electrical outlet) contributed to my eventual development as a psychic.

Shirl began to sense someone "hanging out" along her right side as flashes and a twinkling of lights danced in her peripheral vision. She felt a sense of nausea intermixed with senses of floating or being out-of-body.

Suddenly, an image appeared in the mirrored doorway.

It was the image of a man working in the fields on a farm, or in a rural setting. He was too far away to clearly see his face, but it felt as though it could have been her grandfather. Shirl had learned from the older members of her family that he had been a hardworking man who farmed his own cotton fields in East Texas. Maybe she was imagining what she wished to see, but the accompanying sense of peace and tranquility convinced her it was *real*—at least to her. For some time, she sat mesmerized by the image as the man continued his labor. Then she heard a bell ring—and it was over as suddenly as it had begun.

As Shirl began to regain her connection with the physical environment, she became aware that Dee had entered the room and was standing at the edge of the drawn curtain.

"Are you ready to come out?" Dee whispered.

"Is that why you rang the bell?" Shirl asked.

"What bell?" Dee paused, then smiled and nodded her head as if she understood.

"No, I didn't ring a bell," she said reassuringly, "but people often report that they have heard bells. The forty-five minutes are over. Do you wish to stay or are you finished?"

Shaking her head, Shirl got slowly to her feet. The image was gone, the spell broken.

"It was real. I saw him. We made a connection."

Was It Real?

Who is to say what is real? Reality is defined by the person experiencing it. Shirl made a heartfelt connection and therefore it *was* real to her. She felt complete. She had met her goal. She had experienced a connection with her grandfather.

When she heard the bell ring, all *physical* remnants of her grandfather had disappeared from the room—but the memories and the warm feeling remained . . . .

As did the lyrics of an old Gershwin tune that seemed to be playing over and over in her head:

> *There's a someone I'm longing to see,*
> *I hope that he*
> *turns out to be*
> *someone to watch over me . . . .*[3]

---

3. Gershwin, George. *Someone to Watch Over Me.* Warner Brothers, 1926.

chapter 8

Meeting an Angel

WHAT WAS IT that Shirl experienced in the man-teum? Was it actually the ghostly form of her father? Simply her imagination? Or, perhaps, could it have been her guardian angel providing her with a much needed opportunity for closure?

Spiritual experiences such as Shirl's are more common than you might think. People's lives are often touched by ghosts as well as angels—sometimes, without them even being fully aware of the contact. While ghosts are generally considered to be remnants of souls who have departed the earth, angels are thought to be spiritual forms reflecting or representing the Creator Force. Meeting either of them suddenly can be both a frightening and an awesome experience, to say the least.

According to mainstream Christian thought, angels are beings created by (but separate from) God, existing on a spiritual level above mankind but lower than the Creator. They are believed to be the messengers of God and have not previously incarnated in a physical body. Some Hebrew scholars see them not as independent "beings" but as as direct emanations of God or the Supreme Being, manifested from thought into physical form to deliver a message directly from the Creator. In either case, they are considered to be creations of the Supreme Being, existing to do God's work.

Reports of angels are scattered throughout the Bible. They rescued Daniel from the lions' den and St. Peter from prison. Some theologians attribute the Hebrews' salvation during the Exodus to direct intervention by angels and suggest that these same heavenly forces had a hand in assisting Joshua to bring down the walls of Jericho. They were the apparitions who guided the wise men to Bethlehem. They were the comfort sought by Jesus during his darkest hours.

Of course, not all would agree that their appearance is a guarantee of spiritual deliverance. They seem to test us occasionally, as we can see in the Old Testament story of Abraham and his son at the sacrificial altar. St. Paul actually found them to be wicked according to Ephesians 6, and Revelations 12 tells us that one third of them turned into Satan's demons.

It seems apparent that the appearance of angels did not end in biblical times. Some of history's greatest thinkers, such as Aristotle and Plato, were said to have believed in angels. Socrates often listened to the advice of an angel, whom he referred to as his *daimon*.[1] Angels were the entities that thirteen-year-old Joan of Arc encountered in her father's garden in fifteenth-century France as she was being prepared for her life's journey, and they presented Joseph Smith with the sacred tablets in the early 1800s, leading to the establishment of the Mormon religion.

---

1. Davidson, Gustav. *A Dictionary of Angels*. New York: The Free Press, 1967.

Contrary to what you may assume from the examples above, you don't have to be a key player in determining the fate of the world to see an angel. Countless soldiers in endless wars throughout history have claimed that they owe their lives to intervening angels. Bernadette Soubirious, an ordinary woman, received visions from angels as well as from the Virgin Mary in Lourdes, France in 1858 telling her of the miraculous healing powers of local spring water.[2] Three illiterate children in Fatima, Portugal saw them on May 13, 1917, and large crowds witnessed the miracles that the children subsequently reported would happen.[3] While circling the earth, both Russian and American astronauts have reported seeing angels in space.[4] Billy Graham, the famous evangelist, even wrote a book about them called *Angels: God's Secret Agents* (Doubleday, 1975).

Most people who believe in angels also believe that we each select our own guardian angels before incarnating in physical form. The common belief is that we have at least one and as many as seven guardians—sometimes more. Christian literature is a little less definite about the number of angels in existence. Early Christian writers concluded that there were no more than several hundred in all. By the second century, it was thought that everyone had at least one guardian angel. Then, by the sixth century, Christian scholars held the view that there were nine specific orders or levels of angels. By the Middle Ages, an unidentified writer even claimed to have counted them. According to his figures there were exactly 301,655,722.[5]

2. Krippner & Villoldo. *The Realms of Healing.* Berkeley: Celestial Arts, 1976.

3. Davidson, Gustav. *A Dictionary of Angels.* New York: The Free Press, 1967.

4. Thompson, Keith. *Angels and Aliens.* New York: Fawcett Columbine, 1991.

5. Davidson, Gustav, Op. cit.

The **Angel Experience**

So . . . how do angels communicate with us? One method, of course, is through visions. The Bible provides us with plenty of examples of angelic appearances in physical form. We see them in other ways, too. When we dream, we often have direct contact with our spiritual hierarchy. We can encourage dialogue with them when we incubate a question prior to entering the higher consciousness—the out-of-body experience that we call *sleep*.

They also may actually manifest into physical form to assist us in our hour of need—promptly disappearing when their task has been completed. Take Shirl's and my experience traveling over Donner Summit—a 7,200-foot elevated pass in California, near the Nevada border . . . .

Headed Off (uh, Broken Down) at the Pass

It was late in the afternoon and we had just about reached the top of the grade after a four-hour drive from our home to Lake Tahoe. Suddenly, the dashboard temperature warning light indicated a problem. When we saw steam billowing from under the hood, we knew we had to pull over. As we rounded a tight bend in the road, we came upon a turnout located not far from where the ill-fated Donner party had been stranded by an early snowfall nearly a century before.

Since there were no telephones or sources of water in sight, I lifted the hood and stared at the motor as if *that* was somehow going to resolve the situation. Even for unmechanical me, it was rather easy to determine the problem: steam shooting out of a split in the radiator hose was not defined as "normal" in my seldom-read operator's manual. Because we were stranded on a blind turn on a twisty downhill road, I knew we couldn't expect to get any assistance from a passing motorist.

I opened the back hatch of the car and we rummaged around, searching hopefully for a toolbox and replacement radiator hose that we both knew wasn't there. As I closed the hatch, Shirl noticed a panel truck parked at other end of the pullout, about twenty yards away.

"Where did that truck come from?" Shirl turned to me, puzzled. "It wasn't there a minute ago, was it?"

We both stared in disbelief at the vehicle. We certainly would have seen or heard it pull up and we were both sure that we were alone when we arrived moments before.

"Can I help you?" a voice with a slight British accent inquired, emanating from behind a large boulder near where his truck was parked. "Looks like you are in a bit of a jam, mate."

He was a short black man, probably in his late forties, accompanied by a nice-looking woman carrying a large picnic basket. He walked slowly over to us and glanced under the hood. The woman sat down in the shade of a nearby tree and gently smiled at us.

"Think I blew a hose," I said, returning my attention to the car. I briefly explained what had happened.

"Hmmm," he muttered, then slowly ambled to his panel truck and opened the rear door as if wondering what he might find there.

Following him, I peeked around the edge of the vehicle and into the back. The entire rear of the truck was filled with what might kindly be called "odds and ends." It looked like he had either just come from or was going to a flea market.

He returned to my car and studied the situation more carefully. Glancing through the collection of items that he had loosely spread out, I quickly ruled out the possibility that he happened to have a radiator hose for a six-year-old German sports car in his inventory. I saw no suitcases or clothing to indicate that they were wayfarers and yet, here they were—hanging out at a tourist overlook alongside an interstate highway with what seemed to be a lot of time on their hands. There was no lettering on the side of the vehicle and I quickly concluded, judging by the softness of his hands, that he couldn't possibly be a mechanic.

He came back to his truck, threw me a quick smile, and grabbed an aluminum soft-drink can from the assorted debris. It had some kind of label printed on the side of the container that I didn't recognize. He produced a pair of cutting shears from somewhere beneath the rubble and methodically began to remove the ends of the can. He then cut the remaining cylinder down the side, opening it into one long flat piece of metal. After several minutes of shaping it to his satisfaction, he went around to a side door and extracted a wide roll of black tape from an old cardboard box. He returned to my car and promptly wrapped the split hose with the strip of aluminum and secured it in place with the tape.

"There," he said.

"Do you think it will hold?" I asked tentatively.

"Probably long enough for you to get to a service station," he responded, his clipped British accent sounding oddly out of place.

"Oh . . . this won't work," I muttered. "The nearest station has to be at least ten miles down the road and I'm sure there can't be any water left in my radiator."

"Hmmm . . ." he replied once again, as though pondering why water might be necessary. He then reopened the side door of his truck, which now seemed to have taken on a strange air of magic about it.

"This ought to do," he said, producing two gallon-containers filled with water. He walked to my car and filled the radiator.

"We must be on our way," he said abruptly as he placed the empty containers back into his vehicle. "You should be all set now."

"How can I repay you?" I asked as I reached for my wallet.

"Our pleasure," replied his lady friend, who had reappeared—apparently knowing it was time for them to leave. "Help someone else who needs it," she added as they both climbed into their truck and began to buckle up.

"Wait—" I insisted. "Where do you live? Can I have your address?" I thought the least that I could do was to send them a thank you card or perhaps a certificate for a nice dinner.

He reached into his wallet and pulled out a dog-eared business card that read *Jones Auto* with an address in Berkeley, California.

"Berkeley . . . what a coincidence, that's where my office is," I muttered to anyone near enough to hear. "And you're a *mechanic?*"

"No, not really," he responded softly, his face displaying a quiet smile. The truck began to pull away.

"Jones—his name is *Jones!*" Shirl said excitedly. "That's my maiden name—what a coincidence!" We looked at each other in amazement.

"*Synchronicity,*" we said in unison.

"You're an angel!" Shirl shouted at the departing vehicle. "Thank you!" And then they were out of sight, heading down the mountain.

But that's not the end of the story . . . .

We drove very slowly down the hill toward Truckee, stopping each time the indicator needle began to seriously threaten the little red mark at the end of gauge. About forty-five minutes later, we pulled into one of several large service stations along the freeway. The mechanic who greeted us listened to our story in disbelief, amazed that we managed to get this far with our funky repair.

"Look," Shirl said, "there's the truck! They left ahead of us . . . how did they know which station we would choose?"

"Just wanted to make sure you made it!" our roadside friend shouted, pausing briefly before quickly driving off and out of sight.

Thanks for the Memories

Several weeks later I purchased a nice certificate for a dinner for two and drove to the address on the business card.

There was no such address.

I stopped at the neighboring stores and inquired about the garage. No one had ever heard of it.

I called all the Joneses in the Berkeley telephone directory, but all of my effort was to no avail—our angel had seemingly vanished as magically as he had appeared.

chapter 9

The Art of Psychic Channeling

ALTHOUGH WE HAVE thus far generally categorized
spirit guides and angels as being similar, it might be
helpful for the purists at heart to mention the differences
between them before we continue.

Whereas angels have *not* incarnated in physical form,
spirit guides most definitely have. Also, spirit guides are not
God's messengers. Rather, each guide has a separate function, a distinct energy, and will assist us in differing ways.

Spirit guides appear in many guises, which are
determined by the beliefs of the perceiver. In indigenous cultures, they appear to take on a physical
form and are known by a variety of names
such as leprechauns, *menehunes,*

elves, wee people, or a localized version of an enchanted creature. Others know them as unnamed spirits who, though largely unseen, have the power to influence various aspects of nature, time, and form. For example, Ecuadorian and African shamans see spirit guides as a larger creative force—a union of Mother Earth and nature collectively working as one. Native Americans often perceive them as animal forms who are symbols of spiritual empowerment. Brazilian shamans know them as *orashas*—twelve specific energy forces that are channeled during healing ceremonies.

Most Western metaphysicians perceive spirit guides as personal spiritual entities who, having experienced the physical realm, have graduated to spiritual form. They are thought to be here not only to assist and guide us as individuals, but to work for the benefit of our planet and the universe as a whole.

Besides coming to us through our thoughts, inspirations, or ideas, guides can communicate by directing the movement of a pendulum, influencing the selection of a tarot card or rune, or overseeing the construction of an I Ching hexagram. They may appear in the form of an animal, assisting us with developing the traits that we associate with that particular species. They often communicate by manifesting a recurring symbol to remind us of something we may have over-looked. They might also influence our actions by exposing us to a synchronistic event.

I have four spirit guides. Sami, who channels information when I am reading psychically, resides on my right-hand side. Once I have made a connection with him, I merely open my mouth and the flow of information begins—almost like a reflex action.

My second guide is Joel, the more serious, extremely protective, and moralistic one who hangs out directly above me. He is often dressed in an old-fashioned, ill-fitting suit with socks that seldom match and ties that have been out of style for decades. Joel keeps me on the straight and narrow. He holds me back when my ego gets out of hand.

Amy, my third guide, is a piece of work! I perceive her to be in her late twenties or early thirties. She dresses like a semi-rebel from the sixties. With long hair and a cute figure, she could be a poster girl for perky. She showed up one day on my left, advised me she was here to get me out of my boring rut, then asked if she could put me on hold. I didn't see her for over six months. She balances Joel's conservatism and coaxes me to do things I wouldn't otherwise do, such as speak to large groups of people, host my own TV show—or write this book.

Amy also shelters me from the fear of ridicule. Most psychics fret over the possibility of embarrassing themselves by bombing psychically in front of a large group of people. Amy pumps me up before I go on stage, much like a coach might do for his team prior to a big game. She is my assistant, my confidante, and my biggest fan. When I am about to appear in a public forum, she makes me laugh by shouting *It's showtime!* as we exchange high fives. She's similar to my agent—except she doesn't take fifteen percent off the top.

There is one more spiritual essence positioned behind me who largely remains a mystery. "He" has not allowed me to see him—only to feel his presence. I sense that he is a major player in the metaphysical scheme of things, but he vibrates at a frequency beyond my range of perception.

Psychicism Through the Ages

So how do we develop the skills to actively experience the mysterious non-physical realm of ghosts, spirit guides, and angels? How do we get in touch with this higher knowing that psychics seemingly tap into at will? In order to best understand the process, we need to first take a step back in time ...

In ancient days, the gods spoke through a few select oracles and seers who were highly valued for their ability to foretell the future. One such seer was the Oracle of Delphi,[1] who spoke from a trance while inhaling fumes emanating from a subterranean cavern on what is now the main island of Greece.

---

1. The Oracle of Delphi is briefly discussed on page 60.

Then the mystics and healers proliferated, giving us an extended peek into the unknown. They were the ethereal authorities of individual tribes and settlements across the globe, dispensing cures for the various spiritual and physical ailments of their local societies.

Witches, wizards, and gypsies prevailed in the Middle Ages, dabbling in "magik," spells, and alchemy. They threw the bones, consulted the runes, and interpreted the I Ching. They were feared as much as revered, for their power was said to originate from the mysterious and evil dark side. Others joined secret societies such as the Masons and Rosicrucians, who dabbled in the occult and studied the secret powers of the universe.

Throughout several hundred years of history, spiritualists have delivered messages received from the "other side." Séances were once the order of the day and many sought credible mediums who had the power to contact the departed as well as to peek into the mysteries of the spirit world.

Now, as we approach the new millennium, the question arises: what method has the new age provided? Is there anything beyond traditional methods on the scene?

Some working the spiritual or psychic trade today continue to practice the old traditions, such as reading palms and interpreting the stars. Some psychics enter trances and speak from beyond the physical plane. Others remain conscious, interpreting tarot cards or runes as has been done for centuries. From transcendental wisdom to cosmic harmony, they connect with the non-physical plane by various tried and true methods to provide information or answers. However, in the current era, there *is* something new on the scene. Channeling is the modern psychic's art of choice.

What is Channeling?

Channeling is a catch-all word but is generally a process wherein the psychic allows his or her body to be used to deliver a message by or from a separate spiritual source. It's not unlike a pipeline that channels water from its original location to individual areas where it is most needed. Today, the majority of practicing psychics who channel implement one of these three methods (but other methods do exist):

Method 1: Individual Earthly Spirits

This method involves articulating the voice and personality of independent ghosts or spiritual identities currently residing in nonphysical form. The voice, facial expressions and speech patterns of the psychic often change as he or she becomes an aspect of the spirits rendering the information. The personality of the psychic is moved aside and, as a result, he or she remembers little of what is said.

Some of these psychics, such as J. Z. Knight, channel a single entity. Knight is a well-known medium who speaks for Ramtha—a spirit who claims she was last in a physical incarnation on the lost continent of Lemuria. Diana Hoerig, another prominent seer, speaks for Merlin—an archetypal figure from the days of King Arthur and the Knights of the Round Table. On the other hand, Kevin Ryerson, made famous in a few of Shirley MacLaine's books, articulates multiple (yet separate and differing) energies such as Tom McPherson, an irreverent pickpocket with a Irish brogue and John, an Essene scholar with an Aramaic dialect from the time of Christ. During their healings, Brazilian shamans use this method to channel the personality and medical prowess of famous deceased physicians.

Method 2: The Collective Consciousness

This method of channeling differs from the first in both the way the information is delivered and who it's coming from. Let's use the pipeline analogy. In the first method, the channeled entity is the water in the pipeline—the psychic is in direct contact with a specific individual spirit, who speaks through them. In this second example, the entity is the pipe itself, drawing information from a collective pool and delivering it via the psychic. In this method, the physical plane psychic is in contact with the collective spiritual consciousness.

To accomplish this, the psychic allows a spiritual essence (often identified as a spirit guide, power animal, angel, or a similarly identifiable essential quality) to speak using their voice. Essentially, they tap into a "database" of collective spiritual consciousness rather than receiving information from a specific physical soul or earth-bound identity. As in Method 1, the psychic remains somewhat removed from the event and is often unable to recall much of what is said. Inspired individuals such as artists, musicians, writers, and inventors often, in effect, channel by this method when they employ their creative abilities.

Those who profess a belief in these conduit spirit forms usually describe them as advanced or elevated spiritual energies from whom we requested assistance before we incarnated on this planet. They are often perceived in human form, although they are also commonly encountered as power animals or nature spirits.

Their primary purpose is to protect, guide, encourage, and nurture us as well as provide information for our personal well-being and spiritual growth. They are often the source of our inspirations, ideas, and the spiritual messages or warnings we sometimes confuse as our own thoughts.

An example of a well-known psychic who channels through her spirit guidance is Taryn Krive. Her principal guide identifies herself as a Hopi Indian woman named Barking Tree. The information she delivers is for the purpose of providing clarity and understanding of present-day reality as it applies to the lives of Krive's individual clients.

Others work with multidimensional spirit personalities, like Jane Roberts. She was the first to introduce us to Seth, a spiritual energy claiming to exist simultaneously in the past, present, and future. He sometimes refers to himself as a "dramatization of the unconscious," as quoted in Roberts' book, *Seth Speaks* (Prentice Hall, 1972). He is channeled by more than one psychic, but provides a consistent point of view regarding existence on both the physical and spiritual planes.

I channel implementing this method as well. As in counting by rote or reciting a poem, I don't think of what to say. I just set the entire process on cruise control and see where it takes me.

As I've mentioned previously, the spiritual entity who acts as my conduit is known to me as Sami. Although he is not in a physical body form, that's how I perceive him. It seems that he has a personality and a distinct appearance in order that I might identify his specific energy from my other three guides, who have different functions. When I channel, the information is delivered from my client's guidance directly to Sami, who then relays it through my voice.

I don't edit or judge what is received—it is my experience that a spirit never channels information unsuitable for the person toward whom it is directed. I just move out of the way and let it happen, much like a creative or artistic individual who simply expresses their talent.

Method 3: Speaking to Animals

A separate and distinctive third method of channeling includes psychics who profess to have the ability to talk to or through animals. Such a psychic is Neville Rowe, who communicates with what he calls the group consciousness of six specific dolphins at Sea World in San Diego. He claims they bring an environmental message to mankind by way of telepathic vibrations through Neville's subconscious. Hard to believe, you say? Well, let me share a story involving this third category of channeling.

Laurel, a good friend of mine, owns a beautiful quarter horse named Torie. The horse is one-half thoroughbred and was being trained as an event horse until she was badly injured in a barn accident. The vet determined that the injury was to Torie's hip, necessitating a year or more of treatment and confinement to her stall and paddock.

After two years, Torie still had not shown signs of significant improvement, in spite of the veterinarian's indication that her injury had been properly diagnosed and was healed. For this reason, Laurel decided to transfer her to a breeding farm where she would be allowed to roam freely in a large field. Still, in spite of repeated attempts to breed her, Torie did not produce a foal.

One day when Laurel was visiting Torie, she met a woman claiming to be a psychic who possessed the ability to talk to animals.

"Maybe you could find out why Torie never became pregnant," Laurel said, half jokingly.

"Sure—which one is she?" the psychic responded, looking quite serious. Laurel pointed Torie out from the other horses. With a nod of her head, the psychic walked slowly toward the corral and over to the animal. Then Laurel observed them sauntering around the barn, as two friends might do who wished to have a private conversation.

After about twenty minutes, Laurel's curiosity got the best of her. She peeked around the corner of the enclosure to see what was happening. The psychic was positioned next to Torie, gesturing with her hands as if deep in conversation. The psychic had her back to Laurel, so she couldn't tell if the woman was speaking or using mental telepathy, but the horse was standing quite still as if listening intently. Soon, the psychic motioned to Laurel, indicating she had some answers.

"Are you aware she doesn't like to be confined?" the psychic asked.

"Yes," laughed Laurel. "Whenever she's locked in her stall, she finds a way of getting out. We call her our escape artist."

"It's because of the accident," the psychic continued. "She doesn't like to be in what she kept referring to as 'jail.' She says she was restrained while convalescing, but prefers it here at the breeding farm because she's allowed to roam free."

As Laurel walked with the psychic toward her car, the woman related details about the accident and treatment that was not available to anyone at the farm.

"She insists that she doesn't want to get pregnant," the psychic finished, "—not while her back hurts."

"It was her hip that was injured," replied Laurel.

"Her back," repeated the psychic. "She asked that she be taken off all medication and allowed to rest and remain unencumbered.

"By the way, she likes being a horse," the psychic added as she climbed into her car. "She was a horse in a past life and liked being a mother. She wants to do that again."

Laurel followed the psychic's advice. Soon after, Torie produced two beautiful and healthy colts!

chapter 10

Psychic Tools for Divination

IT IS IMPORTANT to understand that there are many tools one may utilize when developing their inherent psychic ability. Since all psychic experiences involve the process of allowing the truth to flow through us in some form or another, the only thing required is to discover what works best for you. The truth is out there ... all you need to do is to open your preexisting personal channel to it!

When I initially began to hone my psychic skills, I studied palmistry, an ancient (and surprisingly accurate) method of ascertaining the purpose of one's life. I was taught that one hand describes what your spirit initially planned to accomplish during your physical incarnation on this planet, and the other reports the results and potentials once you've committed to a direction.

It didn't take me long to discover that I could not depend *entirely* on the physical lines in the hand to provide a complete message. There are clues in the lines, to be certain, but reputable palmists interpret what they discover and massage it until they speak more from inner knowing than outer observation.

Astrology is another popular metaphysical art for providing and interpreting personal information. It is an ancient system of knowledge based on studying the patterns and movement of the stars and then correlating them to the specific time and place an individual is born into physical existence. It does not predict the future as much as provide insight regarding the best time to address personal growth issues.

Astrology, like palmistry, requires interpretation. For example, many feel that the star of Bethlehem announcing Christ's birth did not *physically* move across the sky. Instead, they suggest, the wise men *read* its meaning using the practice of astrology.

There are many other available tools out there with which you might want to experiment, such as the I Ching, runes, or tarot cards.

Making and Using Tarot

Probably the most popular and widely used divination tool is tarot cards. They work in much the same manner as runes or the I Ching. Tarot is a wonderful implement, as it combines synchronicity (with regard to which card is selected) and the psychic interpretation of the symbols displayed thereon. As is true of palmistry or astrology, to utilize the full potential of this process, one should not entirely depend on the literal meaning of the physical images that appear in the illustrations.

Since there are many types of cards on the market, I am often asked which ones I recommend. My answer is to use whatever works for you. There are simple, easy-to-interpret decks out there for the beginning student as well as complex, esoteric ones for the more advanced reader.

A Deck of Your Own

Some people actually report greater success creating their own tarot cards. They cut out interesting photos in newspapers and magazines and mount them on individual pieces of construction paper to form their own deck.

If you plan to make your own cards, attempt to create as much diversity in the images you select as possible. Choose representations from photos or drawings illustrating a variety of animals, people, landscapes, and objects showing a diversity of contrasting moods. Included, for example, might be a pleasant scene depicting a family celebration contrasted with one portraying the loneliness and isolation of a sad, forgotten individual. Some can be dramatic and full of action while others are bland and pensive. Each tells a story. Each has a message.

Then, when you are searching for clarity regarding a specific issue, you can direct your left (or feminine) hand to select a card or cards, sight unseen. The choice, once studied, may provide insight regarding a specific question or furnish general guidance regarding your life as a whole. You might select one card that provides a direct and immediate answer. Perhaps you will isolate several that require quiet contemplation through long-term meditation. All of this may depend on your intention, your mood, or your intuition in the moment as well as the complexity of the subject or concern.

Some prefer the "one card method," immediately going for the bottom line. This might be useful for a less complicated situation or one requiring immediate action. Others will choose multiple cards in order to ascertain or reflect on a deeper meaning. This procedure can be facilitated by drawing the initial card to identify the subject or issue to be revealed or resolved. The subsequent "supporting" cards can be drawn in pairs to provide insight into 1) what has prevented you from obtaining your goals and 2) what can assist you in your growth; or perhaps, 1) what has restricted you in the past and 2) what can support you in the future.

I often use a deck of cards that illustrates simple objects such as a pond of water, a tree, a bird, a coil of rope, a nail, etc. I might ask, for example: What is my life purpose or issue? What is holding me back and what will aid my completion?

A Sample Reading

Let's say I drew cards depicting a tree, a bird and a nail. I might interpret them according to my own personal associations about the symbols, as follows:

> *First question:* What is my life purpose or issue?
> *First card:* Tree
> *Analysis:* What is a tree and how does it relate to my question? For me, a tree represents something powerful It is long lasting and grows slowly. As it correlates to my question, I might conclude that my life purpose involves a major, slow-growing, powerful issue. My purpose might be to address my long-term personal spiritual growth.

> *Second question:* What is holding me back?
> *Second card:* Bird
> *Analysis:* What is a bird? My view is that it is something that flies free and soars above things. I might ask myself (with the knowledge that I am responsible for all that happens to me) what is it that I am doing that is limiting my ability to soar— particularly in relation to the issue revealed by the first card and my question pertaining to life purpose. Maybe I'm not being "free" enough in my thinking. Perhaps my actions do not allow me to "fly" beyond self imposed limitations and fears. I might want to meditate on that one for further enlightenment.

Third question: What is aiding my growth?

Third card: Nail

Analysis: What is a nail? I might conclude that it is something one has to target when swinging a hammer, or something that joins or connects other things together. Maybe I need to be more specific about my target or my focus. Perhaps it is in my best interest to join several concepts together or to be less scattered. Possibly I am being instructed to keep "hammering" at the problem or concern that was revealed in the first card.

It is important to note that your answers are yours alone and are not to be interpreted or judged by others. For example, you may not come to the same conclusions regarding the meanings of the specific symbols on the cards as I did. When you select your card, *your* truth is before you. You become your own psychic and discover your individual truth through your personal and unique impressions.

Okay, now that we know how to work with the cards, you might wonder why or how the cards we select at random have anything to do with providing insight or legitimate answers to any question.

Ah . . . glad you asked. It is a process known as *synchronicity.*

Synchronicity is No Coincidence

Synchronicity is a concept that we often confuse with coincidence. *Coincidence,* as defined by *Webster's New World Dictionary,* is "an accidental and remarkable occurrence of events or ideas at the same time." It suggests that coincidental events lack anything more than a casual relationship to each other.

Synchronicity, we are informed in the same reference book, means "simultaneous occurrences" and suggests that situations or events are often interconnected beyond a random accident or coincidence. As Peggy, a good friend of mine, coincidentally stated in a doctoral paper she is preparing on synchronicity, synchronicity can best be recognized and utilized when "acting or seeing from a place of intuition rather than from a place of logically pre-planned actions." This suggests that with regard to our perception, *nothing is accidental.* Everything has greater meaning in the grand scheme of things.

When we better understand this concept, we begin to be privy to a larger view of the issues and events that constantly take place around us. We soon realize that everything that occurs supports a common theme and pertains, on some level, to our spiritual growth.

Consider the tarot cards. If you can learn to trust in "synchronistic random selection," you may be provided useful insight or information about your situation that you might not otherwise discover. If this is true, might not this process be valuable on a larger scale in relation to our daily lives? The chance encounter with a friend who provides you with timely information . . . the unsolicited catalog wherein you find a needed item . . . the incorrect information that leads to a new opportunity . . . .

In order to benefit from synchronicity, we must first let go of the left-brain actions of Mr. Control. The deeper we commit to opening to our intuition, the greater the likelihood that the process of synchronicity will be free to function. *Intent* is the key ingredient. When our heart (intention) and mind (action) are in alignment, synchronicity has a better chance of operating successfully.

Manifest What You Want

Once we learn how to recognize the synchronicity occurring all around us, we can use our insight to manifest whatever it is that we require to bring closure to an uncertainty or problem. When we know what we need (clarity and focus), know in our hearts that it is possible (intention) and then let go of the limitation (fear), we can create the desired outcome. This is a metaphysical law of nature, no different in its necessity to operate than Newton's law of gravity or perpetual motion. Sometimes the results are instantaneous and sometimes they are slow to materialize, but if you utilize the tools at your disposal, events will have been undeniably set into motion to create either your requested conclusion or the learning experience required to complete your education.

So—be careful what you ask for, because chances are you're going to get it. As the mystics and sages have stated for centuries, the universe is just an illusion . . . why not create it the way you want it to be?

The Luck of the Draw

You might be wondering: How does synchronicity work in our every-day lives? Well, here's an example. Several years ago Shirl and I, along with two friends, were vacationing on the big island in Hawaii. We were staying in a hotel that conducted a random drawing each day to select a few guests who would be given the opportunity to swim with their resident dolphins. Dolphins and whales, as you might know, are considered by metaphysicians to be very special creatures. Whether their ethereal essence originates from the deep reaches of space or they are simply pure spiritual mammals, metaphysicians who communicate with them generally agree that they are extremely intelligent mammals assisting us in our efforts to save the planet.

For the day we would be available, the chances of being selected were statistically minuscule. As expected, when the names were drawn, none of the four of us were included. However, we decided to wander down to the entrance to the lagoon and inquire about our chances of being added to a waiting list should the selected parties not appear.

"You've got to be kidding," was the reply from the young lady behind the counter at the check-in desk. "When people sign up for the drawing, you can pretty much count on them appearing if selected," she said. "We draw six names along with ten alternates for each session—your chances are *somewhat* remote," she added with a sympathetic chuckle.

Still, we decided to hang around—and unbelievably, when it was time to begin the morning session, only three of the selected winners and alternates had appeared to fill the six available positions.

There were three openings.

Shirl and I had previously agreed that our friends were to be given priority should the opportunity occur and I insisted that my wife take the third and last slot, if available.

"This has never happened before," the beach director reported. "What a coincidence."

"Synchronicity," I muttered as my wife and I just looked at each other and smiled.

Swimming with the dolphins turned out to be an awesome experience. It began with the six lucky participants sitting on a float in water up to their chests, emotionally connecting with the dolphins as they cautiously approached. Then, one by one, the mammals would place their heads in the lap of one of the human participants and establish eye contact. Eventually, each person was allowed to slowly slip into the water and, for the next hour or so, swim alongside these magnificent creatures.

Naturally, I was pleased for my wife and friends but disappointed that I couldn't take part in the experience. When they returned from the lagoon, they spoke glowingly of their adventure and the combined energy of the three of them would have blinded the most neophyte of psychic practitioners. All agreed that I had to join the afternoon session.

Fat chance, I thought.

"Hey, aren't you the one who always speaks of creating your desired reality?" asked our friend Barbara, who was still radiant from her experience.

"Yeah, why not just ask the Fate Guy?" teased her husband, for whom the subtleties of parapsychology had never been firmly accepted. For him, "synchronicity" and "fate" were interchangeable words, and who was I to attempt to convince him otherwise?

After lunch, we returned to the booth to ascertain what my chances might be for participating in the afternoon session. Unfortunately, the area was crowded with many others who had the same idea. When I reached the counter, I signed up on the waiting list . . . as number *twelve*.

When the afternoon program was about to begin, only five of the winners and alternates were present.

"Strange . . . " muttered the bikini-clad director. She then ripped up a number of pieces of paper and placed them into a beach hat. She asked each of the twelve of us on the waiting list to select one.

"Whoever picks the one with the hotel name written on it may assume the sixth and last position," she announced.

When it was my turn to draw, several of the slips had already been taken. The beach director smiled at me—probably sympathetically rooting for me since she knew that I was the only one of the four of us traveling together who had been excluded from that morning's session.

I reached into the hat. I noticed that the ballot in my hand looked slightly different than the others.

I don't think so, whispered Amy, one of my four spirit guides. She had always been the most playful of spiritual helpers. I hadn't considered calling on my guides to assist me in selecting the winning slip of paper, since I had painfully learned my lesson in Reno not to rely on my psychic gift for personal benefit if it is done at the expense of others. At that time, I decided to try to make a little money at the gambling tables because, if I could use this "power" to determine what was going to happen ahead of time, I could probably retire with a large bank account in less than a few days time.

Instead, I left with a depleted checkbook.

No, not that one either, Amy suggested quietly.

So, I just closed my eyes and trusted my hand to go where it wanted to go. I selected a slip and opened it slowly.

"Congratulations!" trumpeted the director, winking coyly at me. "It looks like you're the winner!"

I glanced at my wife and friends who were both ecstatic and relieved that I would be able to share their awesome experience.

Whether the attendant had positioned the basket to the correct angle or Amy helped with my selection or the Fate Guy was on my side, I don't know—I never asked. I guess there are just some things best left unknown. What I do know is that *synchronicity* played a significant hand in the process.

Oh yeah—and they were right . . . swimming with the dolphins *was* an awesome experience!

chapter 11

Working with Spirit Guides

NOW THAT WE have some tools, let's discuss more specifically what occurs during a psychic reading. What might you expect to experience once you open your psychic channels to this source of information, and how might you do it safely?

The procedures followed by psychics during their readings differ as greatly as the techniques artists and musicians utilize when expressing their individual talents. Those who prefer to demonstrate their extrasensory abilities in a public forum predominately focus on information pertaining to the entire planet or the attending audience as a whole. On the other hand, psychics who choose to work with single clients will generally channel guidance that specifically pertains to the one requesting the session.

I think I can best demonstrate this process by first telling you how "we" work (Sami prefers that I use the word *we* rather than *I*). We do not issue proclamations regarding the whole of mankind. Instead, we prefer to read for individuals or couples, dividing the sessions into four sections. We begin by providing my clients their truth as relayed by their higher source. This information generally addresses such topics as their purpose in this incarnation, why they chose their specific parents, what they're here to accomplish, and what may be standing in the way of their completion of life goals.

From this level of understanding, Sami and I progress into the second phase of the reading—providing insights about pertinent past incarnations and the resultant karma brought forward to this life for resolution through reincarnation.

Virtually all religions portray the Creative Force as being eternal—without beginning and end. Couldn't this also be true of humans? After all, we're said to be molded in the Creator's image. If it's true—if our souls proliferate through eternity—then seeking awareness about our personal process of continually returning to physical existence is a great resource. Learning about a past life can be beneficial in the event that we left some of our work unfinished the last time we were here. It stands to reason that if we know who and where we've been, we might gain insight into where we're headed.

The observable cycle of nature illustrates the principles of reincarnation—namely, that life is both purposeful and continuous. All of nature's creations grow and evolve with time—as do we. Nature has a purpose and direction—as do we. Each season has a beginning and an ending—as do we. The earth's beginnings and ends are not final. They are part of a larger cycle, and will occur again and again—naturally. We are no different.

- Spring is the season when new life comes forth and struggles to survive. Likewise, a baby is born into a new life and it, too, struggles to endure.

- ◆ The season changes to summer when nature grows into fullness. In the same manner, a child grows into its adult life and develops into the fullness of its being.

- ◆ Fall follows summer and is the time of harvest. Similarly, as we grow older, we begin to reap the consequences—the harvest—of our lifetime.

- ◆ Winter completes the orbit and life becomes dormant, only to return again at season's end as a new seed grows into a new form. At the end of a human lifetime, the body dies—but the spiritual essence returns once again by way of new seed in a new form.

The Big Bang theory, describing the creation of the universe, reflects this cyclical life rhythm. Our scientists inform us that the universe began with a single mass of expanding energy that one day will begin to collapse on itself, only to repeat the entire process once again. We, too, are born, expand into our fullness, die, and are born again, continuing the cycle.

Just as we reflect the sum of our experiences in *this* lifetime, our current life reflects the compiled experiences of *past* lives. We all know that if we review our recent mistakes, we can profit by the lessons learned. In the same manner, a psychic review of our past lives may provide understanding regarding the perceived struggles and difficulties brought forth into this one. This comprehension can be of enormous value to one wishing to grow and advance spiritually.

In the third phase of Sami's and my reading, we respond to questions the client has brought us. No question is inappropriate, of course, and each is addressed befitting the best interests of the one asking. Answers pertaining to the future outcome of a situation are often directed more toward understanding the karmic lesson being presented than to a specific solution to the problem. Generally, the majority of the client's questions are answered in the previous two phases of the reading—before they've even been asked.

Our reading concludes by introducing the client to their higher source of knowing. Whether we wish to refer to this source as individual spirit guides, a higher consciousness, a guardian angel, or some aspect of the Supreme Being, it all basically originates from the Source—universal life energy. The fact that it is a reference to our individual truth is the important thing.

Get to Know Your Guides

By perceiving these spiritual energy guides as a physical-like form, each person who is willing to trust the channeling process is generally provided some sort of mental picture with which (or with whom) to communicate. Since each spirit guide has a different and distinctive gift to bring to the mix, each is perceived as a unique personality corresponding to a distinct visual form. Just as a dentist provides a different expertise than an auto mechanic, each guide provides a special and unique quality to life.

Our guides communicate with us constantly, whether we are aware of them or not. Once we begin to request their assistance, we can consciously benefit from their wisdom and strength. They work in many ways, such as through our meditations, in our dreams, or by arranging "coincidences" or synchronistic events in our waking life. They are responsive to both our spoken requests and silent needs.

We receive the greatest benefit, of course, when we consciously pay attention to our guides. After all, if we wish to be informed about events occurring in our world, we don't just sit around wondering about it all—we tune into our radio or television, or we purchase a newspaper. Furthermore, if we desire specific information such as local weather conditions, we listen to a *particular* radio or television station or consult a defined section in our newspaper. True, we will absorb some information by happenstance, but until we make the effort to consult an informed authority, we cannot fully access the extensive data available to us.

The beautiful thing about consulting our spirit guides is that *all we have to do is to ask.*

Before we begin actively seeking spiritual contact, it is helpful to know the answer to two important questions. First, how do we safely go about seeking this understanding? Second, what might we encounter along the way?

How to Safely Seek Spiritual Understanding

If you require a long, detailed explanation about how to get in touch with this higher truth, you can consult ancient charts, mystic writings, and complex graphs. I can introduce complicated theory and evolved quantum logic and then suggest you commit to a lifetime of study. This path will most likely necessitate seeking a variety of gurus; complete immersion in a remote monastery, convent, or religious community; and full-time dedication to reading volumes of books.

Or, if you prefer a short concise answer, all you need are three words: *Just do it.*[1]

Meditation

If you wish a simple means by which to explore this vast realm of esoteric knowledge, consider exploring the simple concept of meditation. It is a basic and direct means of accessing higher consciousness in order to manifest what you desire.

> *Question:* What is meditation?
> *Answer:* It is simply quieting the mind, being still and observing what happens next.

That sounds pretty straightforward, doesn't it?

> *Question:* How is it valuable?

---

1. A slightly longer version might be: *Know* that it is possible—know that you can do it!

Answer: Meditation may produce a range of results—from specific answers to your questions or to the discovery of inner peace and a connection to the higher Source.

Fairly desirable benefits, wouldn't you say?

Question: How is this done?

Answer: Meditation can be accomplished by many means beyond the stereotypical fashion of being seated in the lotus position while burning incense and chanting a mantra. Sitting next to the ocean is a form of meditation. Listening to your favorite music with closed eyes is a form of meditation. Being seated in a black box waiting for the form of your deceased grandfather is a form of meditation.

The only commitment here is time and desire. Oh yeah—and to know that you can do it!

So, what happens when we meditate? Not unlike our reaction to hypnosis, we tend to drift from what we term "ordinary" conscious reality into a semi-subconscious, relaxed, tension-free, trance-like state. By shifting into the perspective of an observer, we become objective—connected to a deeper knowing. From this unattached perspective, we can often perceive our truth more clearly. It is here that we can ask questions and begin to seek answers. It is here that we can search for objectivity, freedom, and peace of mind. It is here that we can seek the purpose of our existence. It is here that we learn to listen to our inner truth.

Sounds pretty good so far, doesn't it?

What Might We Encounter Along the Way?

When we go about seeking answers to our questions or looking for the doorway to nirvana . . . what could we come across? The concise, bottom line answer is: It depends on our intention.

We need to be clear about our intention when reaching out to this higher Source. What is our motivation? Is it personal wealth, quick and easy solutions, or control of others? Are we seeking a shortcut? Do we wish to gain physical resources at the expense of others? If so, then the karma you might assume will negate any short-term advantage—believe me.

If, instead, you are seeking personal growth or spiritual evolution, you may have found an effective tool. However, as we enter the world of spirit, there are a variety of manifestations we might encounter, including our spiritual guidance, a departed relative, a wayward negative force, or a past-life memory.

For example, if Shirl's intentions weren't clear when she entered the manteum, she might have experienced any of the following scenarios:

- ◆ She could have met one of her spiritual guides, angels, or power animals who, as has been said, are here to assist us in completing our past-life karma and exploring our full physical potential.

- ◆ She may have met a familiar spirit with whom she had karma.

- ◆ She might have discovered a not-so-friendly negative energy whose selfish agenda was to sap her strength for its own selfish purposes.

- ◆ She may have viewed one of her own past lives in the form of a *déjà vu* experience or soul memory.

- ◆ She could have witnessed a life review, as is said to occur during the dying process.

When soliciting guidance or inspiration, we always want to meditate first, or acknowledge the Creator Force. Next, we need to focus our intention on what we are seeking for our spiritual growth. This simple act opens the doorway to higher thought and begins the process of manifesting that which supports our higher purpose and personal truth. The more we connect and are absorbed into this spiritual energy, the less influence our ego and personal fear will have on our experience. This process also tends to close the door to other, less desirable, energies that might be hanging out in the ether.

Be specific about your desires and always request *only* the information that is in your best interest to obtain. As the Bible tells us— ask, and you shall receive.

Several outcomes are possible once you solicit specific assistance from your spirit guides:

- ◆ Occasionally you will be provided a direct message, complete with multiple possibilities from which you can pick and choose.

- ◆ Sometimes you will receive a more subtle inspiration or thought and it will be up to you to develop it into actualization.

- ◆ Most often you will be led in a specific direction and it will be up to you to find your own answers. After all, if they tell you where the eggs are, the Easter egg hunt becomes boring, doesn't it?

When I was being confronted with a changing business environment as the president of my construction company, I relied on a form of meditation to direct me to the proper path to pursue. I didn't ask how to make more money, or even how to deal with the competition. Instead, I requested clarity regarding what positive steps to follow so that my employees and I might gain freedom from the overwhelming stress we were experiencing.

The answer I received was quite unexpected. I was being counseled to close down the business. At the time, my rational mind considered this to be both an illogical and unacceptable conclusion. How would I survive? What about the company employees? Would I have failed?

I realized that the guidance I received through the meditation was correct when synchronistic events began to support the spiritual directives. My gut provided the final confirmation.

It turned out to be the best possible direction I could have taken.

By surrounding ourselves in the white light of spiritual love and directing our intentions to a specific purpose, we can insure that we are being connected to the party with whom we intend to speak.

But first we have to make sure we dial the correct area code . . . .

chapter 12

How to Contact Your Guides

WOULD YOU LIKE to meet *your* spirit guides? If so, I recommend that you begin by selecting the appropriate space and creating a ceremony suitable for the initial meeting. Doing *anything* ceremoniously enhances the importance of the experience, so planning a special ritual for a "spiritual happening" is certainly appropriate.

Being a minister, I can perform a simple marriage in an ordinary room with nothing more than a single witness and a few select words. However, I can also officiate a grand celebration in an elegant setting, complete with ample food and drink, festive music, and meaningful formality, all witnessed by a large gathering of loving and supportive friends. The government considers you just as married either way, but the magic created by pomp and circumstance and a proper setting seems to somehow make the commitment more binding.

Preparing the Site

A good location to develop your initial contact with your guidance is in a quiet, out-of-the-way area of your dwelling or yard. Better yet, find a secluded place in the sacred reaches of nature. My favorite kind of location is a circle of trees or rocks in a peaceful natural setting in the high desert or mountains. Being near water, whether it be a small lake or a massive ocean, is a wonderful spiritual setting as well.

If you researched the original locations of the world's most sacred sites, you would discover that they were often at the top, center, or apex of a natural earth formation. However, few physical remnants of these sites remain in existence today, having been obliterated by expanding cities or replaced by grandiose religious edifices constructed by successive conquering nations.

Once you have selected or located your sacred site, approach it with clear spiritual intent. Honor the ground in some way, by planting a tree, burying one of your favorite crystals, or by singing or chanting. Even the act of picking up discarded trash littering the immediate vicinity is befitting of the energy of your special space.

Those who regularly live and worship in nature honor its sacredness. In my experience, the only glowing exception to this rule were the natives in the Ecuadorian rain forests—and it turned out that they weren't much of an exception after all. We couldn't believe our eyes when we observed these people carelessly dropping candy wrappers in their sacred environment. Such blatant disrespect of nature seemed outrageous until we learned that wrapped candy was new to them and they never even remotely considered that mankind would produce something that was not biodegradable. Everything in their primitive life experience is simple, mutually shared, and recycled back to nature.

Isn't it ironic that it is often the "better educated" and "intelligent" of our species, living in the modern Western world, who are the most irreverent when it comes to our natural resources?

Honoring the Chosen Location

If possible, you should initially approach your sacred space by first walking its perimeter in a counterclockwise direction. This process tends to honor the entire space, much as Native Americans do when they first offer tribute to the elements and the directions on the medicine wheel before beginning their rituals. This movement also establishes the flow of energy in an upward spiral, opening the path to the Creator Force.

An example of how this spiral works exists in a grand church containing no pews or chairs in its cavernous sanctuary in the capital city of Brazil. As you enter this most sacred space, you encounter a large spiral painted on the floor. Rather than sitting passively through a religious service, the worshiper in this space embarks on a spiritual journey, following the spiral round and round, counterclockwise, until it delivers him or her into the center. Once there, the worshiper meditates beneath what is said to be the largest mined crystal in the world.

Extending beyond the roof into the sunlight, the giant crystal reflects and refracts light into the church sanctuary, providing visual and subtle spiritual light in a most inspiring manner. Later, when your devotional efforts have been completed, you spiral in a clockwise direction, a grounding process that brings you back to "reality."

Making a Sacred Circle

Once you have located your sacred space, evaluate its boundaries. If the outer boundaries are not in the form of a circle, then create one, implementing nearby rocks or stones. Circles are important in most indigenous cultures as they have no beginning and no end. Being the aspect of infinity and limitlessness, they represent the ultimate in spirituality and the Creator Force. Native Americans, for example, believe that the power of the world works through a circle or sacred hoop. After all, the earth and stars are round, the universe moves in circles, and the wind in its greatest power whirls. The seasons always come full circle, too, returning to where they started.

Preparing Yourself

The first thing you need to do to prepare yourself for spiritual communication is to ground yourself. Grounding is a process by which you can come to increased clarity and stay within your power—it will be your next step in preparing to contact your guides. Grounding is the antithesis of being "scattered" and "spacy." So how does one accomplish it?

Getting Grounded

1. Trace the outline of your feet in the dirt to establish your position in the chosen space. Imagine that the soles of your feet are roots of a tree. Visualize them burrowing deeply into the soil.

2. Release all of your limitations, doubts and fears into *Pachamama* to be naturally cleansed and recycled. This is like the process our body follows as it systematically eliminates waste after extracting the necessary nutrients from our food.

3. Since nature abhors a vacuum, draw in positive earth energy to replace the negative energy that has been discarded. Seek the energy-enhancing natural healing, protection, and ancient knowledge that resides in the earth. Imagine these resources being drawn into your body just as a tree pulls water from the ground.

The symbol of the tree is a worthy example here, because hugging a tree is an effective means to ground as well as to receive energy. Hugging a tree allows us to connect to the earth through its roots and "download" all of our spent energy, like outmoded belief systems or restrictive limitations, into the ground to be regenerated. This is a reciprocal process, healthy for both you and the tree—it's not unlike nature's process of turning animal feces into fertilizer. Trees are "yang" (masculine) to our "yin" (feminine).[1] For example: to thrive, they require the carbon dioxide that we exhale, while we require the oxygen that they subsequently produce.

4. When you are receiving energy, cycle the flow—simultaneously replenishing yourself with revitalized energy by filling the same area that is being vacated by the energy you are discarding. One way to accomplish this is to grab two limbs of the same tree and pull in new energy with your left (yin, or receiving) hand as you release the old, spent energy with the right (yang, or sending) hand.

During our travels through the rain forests of Ecuador, we never felt fatigued because we were in a naturally reciprocal environment: the rich, oxygen-producing trees and plants constantly provided the energy we needed to continue our journey.

Protection and Expansion

Now that you are properly grounded, shift your focus to the ethereal light of protection as it descends from the infinite universe above you. Allow this spiritual aspect to envelop you, as you might experience the warming rays of the sun. At the same time, get in touch with your inner-dwelling God essence—a spirituality that resides in your heart chakra. Expand this inner essence outward and allow it to mix with the descending spiritual light.

The consciousness expansion of your inner light is a process that moves with a directed and connected force. Expansion implies *intention*—a word used often throughout this book. Be aware that there is

---

1. Yin and yang are Taoist terms relating to the cosmic harmony that is sought after by balancing the polarities of yin (the sensitive and creative feminine force) and yang (the powerful, ego-driven male force).

a subtle difference between *expansion* of the light and *letting go* of the light. Be sure you are focused on expansion, since "letting go" suggests that you may be discarding energy or abandoning control as you might if you were dumping used or unneeded energy.

When combined, the spiritual light and energy from above and the God essence from within you will form a shielding shell of love around you, providing the proper protective forum for your spirit guides to make themselves known. Think of this shield as a filter, repelling negative energy and fear while providing a good space to attract and increase positive vibrations. Now you're ready . . . .

Opening to Spiritual Communication

You have created your space, grounded, and protected yourself from lingering negative forces. Like the analogy of giving a dinner party, the table is set, the salad is made, and the dinner is in the oven. All you need now are the guests.

By setting the *intention* to connect with your spirit guides, you will connect. Money back guarantee. The only problem you may encounter is *when*. They may appear to you at that very moment by way of a thought or inspiration. You may receive a mental vision a few days later or "hear" a few words as you drift off to sleep a month from now. Or, you may simply begin to feel their presence. Perhaps you'll glance up in the sky and receive an answer from an image in a passing cloud, or discover an enlightening image on a stone near your feet.

If you don't feel connected with your spiritual force following the ceremony, know at least that you've opened the door—you just might not be able to see anything until your third eye adjusts to the spiritual light. It's possible that you have been in denial about spiritual forces for most of your life, and it might require persistence to break through your old belief systems. Understand also that guides sometimes prefer to wait and see just how serious and committed you are about establishing a long-term dialogue. Imagine a friend traveling a great distance at your request only to discover that you do not intend to accept their assistance.

Many people who begin to receive input from their guides never actually "meet" them in the literal sense—they don't see or hear them on the physical plane. Often their guides just arrange for things to happen. The experience is something like writing down a request, mailing it, and enjoying the subsequent benefits in an unexpected form thanks to an unseen source. Seems a little like Christmas morning—after all, we never actually *see* Santa Claus, either, after we've sent him our wish list . . . .

The key word in all of these proceedings is *intention*. It's simple: thought + intention = form.

Once you've achieved the connection with your higher self, you may perceive more than one spirit guide. You could get answers to specific inquiries or encounter information beneficial to your growth or survival without even formally asking a question. You may be presented opportunities to work through karma carried over from past lives, discover a hidden talent, or ascertain your greater purpose.

Every Problem is an Opportunity to Learn

Should you become aware of a recurring problem in your life, you can request that your guidance not only assist you in resolving it, but help you to discover and eliminate the cause. For example, do all of your emotional relationships self-destruct just when you think you've found your permanent partner? Does every attempt to resolve a specific conflict end with the same disappointing results?

Your guides can and will help you to resolve your problems, but remember: communicating with your spirit guides doesn't mean you'll suddenly start living a charmed life. We have all, at one time or another, been placed in uncomfortable situations by our guides for the express purpose of learning a specific lesson. As parents, don't we use the same process with our children? Don't we reconstruct problems in order to provide our kids opportunities to learn? Don't we harp on the same issues until they finally learn whatever it is that we wish to teach them?

If you are experiencing a recurring problem, don't ask to have it eliminated—rather, ask your guidance to assist you in identifying your lesson. Once you ascertain the issue at hand (the reason you are constantly being given the problem), let your guides know what you have discovered. When they are convinced that you have learned the lesson, they will no longer continue to present it. This is no different than been held after school by your teacher—once you understand your lesson, you are free to go out and play.

Be Persistent

Often we are tested to see how much desire we have. Sometimes we have to insist that we want to be heard. Occasionally, we may even have to shout.

Shirl, for example, needed all the persistence she could muster during the darkest days of her daughter's illness. After running into one major frustration after another, she ventured into our backyard and literally shouted at her spirit guides. She complained that she had been manifesting like crazy but she could not discern any progress in the proper diagnosis and treatment of her daughter's elusive disease. She had what she called "a real heart-to-heart talk" with them. She knew she couldn't change what had already been set in motion by the "Fate Guy," but she needed to discover and process whatever lessons they wished she or her daughter to learn so that they might both move on with the rest of their lives. As a result of her intense determination, her daughter's illness was soon properly diagnosed and eventually eliminated.

Be Specific and Focused about What You Want

Always communicate to your higher self the specifics of what it is that you really desire. For example, if you are marooned on a deserted island, don't ask your guides for money to buy a boat. After all, there may not be anyone available to sell one to you. Don't even request a boat—you may get one without fuel or power.

Ask to get off the island!

Your choices are conditioned by your experiences. They are limited compared to those available to the universe. Have your goal in mind, and let the universe take care of the details.

How can Santa bring exactly what you want—unless you ask for it?

chapter 13

Threatened by a Ghost

IS IT REALLY possible to encounter a ghost when seeking to meet your angel or spirit guide? Could we possibly rendezvous with an unfriendly spirit while attempting closure with a departed relative? Is there some action we can take when we sense negative or foreboding energy nearby? The answer to all of these questions is *yes*.

When Shirl sat in the black box, she could have easily encountered a not-so-friendly spirit instead of her grandfather. Because of this possibility, she first established protection for herself by expanding the white light of love around her body. Then she took the equally important step of carefully setting her intention regarding her expectations.

By expanding the white light of love around her, Shirl was able to provide a positive protective field of energy to ward off any negative vibrations seeking a host on which to anchor. By making her intention clear, she set the tone for what was to follow.

Our intentions and expectations are thoughts. Since all thought is pure energy, and since all energy that is set into motion creates our reality, the inevitable conclusion is that our reality is the manifestation of our intentions and expectations.

To put it simply, our expectations *become* our reality.

If Shirl had attempted to contact her grandfather primarily to fulfill her ego or enhance her personal power, the outcome could have been quite different. Soliciting his attention after all this time for the sole purpose of satisfying her curiosity might have created some negative karma between them.

Since her grandfather had been absent from the physical realm for many years (although purists will point out that time is a concept that does not apply in the spirit world), recalling him could have been potentially disruptive to his spiritual journey. However, Shirl was certain that her grandfather had initiated contact and Pai Ely, our Brazilian shaman houseguest, had definitely concurred. For this reason, Shirl's intention to complete the spiritual circuit was not inappropriate.

What Are Ghosts?

Ghosts, also known as phantoms or apparitions, are generally the non-physical spirits of a living person or animal who has died. Occasionally a ghost is the remaining energy of a highly charged object—a lingering influence after the object has been destroyed. "Ghost ships" or other mysteriously reappearing objects are examples of such a phenomenon. Although sometimes "seen" by the naked eye or in photographs, ghosts are most often merely sensed by those who are open to the extrasensory perceptions of clairvoyance (vision), clairaudience (sound), or clairessence (feeling).

Ghosts differ from spirit guides in that they were not selected by you to assist you in fulfilling your destiny for this life and they do not necessarily uphold your spiritual growth as a top priority. They are often tied to a place for reasons stemming from their own earthly incarnation, and may contact you for any number of reasons—some positive, some negative.

The Characteristics of Ghostly Contact

As a general statement, the longer a spirit energy is gone from the physical plane, the more difficult it is for it to return to, let alone communicate with, our corporeal world. Like a memory, the further back in time you venture, the more difficult it is to accurately recreate or connect with the original energy. Although linear time is not relevant to the spirit world, it does exist here—in the physical world—and for Shirl's grandfather to be attempting contact after all this time was most unusual.

If a departed relative wants to communicate with you, the attempted contact will most likely occur during the first year or so of their transition. They may appear to you in many forms and in various ways—possibly in the guise of a physical ghostly apparition, speaking or motioning to you. Sometimes they will approach as a comforting thought when you are in an emotional moment of need. The unexpected discovery of a misplaced letter or the timely playing of their favorite song might signal their presence. And, of course, a dream is a familiar and comfortable environment conducive to such a connection.

They often appear around meaningful days such as birthdays, anniversaries, holidays, or a special day when the loved one is strongest in our thoughts. For the most part, these are friendly and loving experiences that are often initiated for the purpose of providing comfort, assurance, or closure—particularly if the loved one's departure was sudden or unexpected. A ceremony at a power site or location that holds special memories for the two of you can be a positive and healthy experience. On the other hand, holding the departed soul here by excessive grief and dependency is not fair to either of you.

Jim, a good friend of mine, received a series of strong impressions of his dad nearly twelve months after his father had died. At first, Jim was hesitant to share this experience with me. He wasn't sure if it was a hallucination or just a strong memory triggered near the anniversary of his dad's passing. When I questioned him further, he said that he didn't receive any verbal information, yet felt relieved because his dad looked "radiant."

"I didn't see him with my eyes," he insisted, "yet I clearly knew he was there."

As I explained to Jim, ghostly energy is often mistaken for a memory, a passing feeling, or even an ordinary dream. They may come to deliver the message that they are okay or that they love you—or perhaps they'll request your forgiveness. Regardless of the method they use to implement contact, you will process and understand the "impression" by whatever means is most natural and with which you feel most comfortable.

If you experience such a contact, inform the spirit that you sense or feel them. If the energy is positive, they are most likely providing approval or support. I am reminded of a woman I know whose deceased husband returned several times in her dreams to provide his endorsement of her relationship with another man—a relationship she was uncertain about beginning.

So . . . if you are unsure whether your encounter is real or imagined, encourage the spirit to communicate more clearly with you. Set your intention and extend your light. Hey, you never know if or when you will be able to receive a message from them again.

Of course, it's natural to be apprehensive about completing the circuit with the spirit of a departed loved one, particularly if this entire concept is new to you. However, the comfort and peace of mind gained by such an encounter can be most beneficial. Not only might you receive the assurances you seek from the "other side," but your expanded understanding of what takes place during and after the death process will tend to minimize the fear around *your* eventual transition.

It is said that when we leave this physical body, our experience will parallel our expectations. Those who have died and returned confirm this concept. What better way to prepare for our own journey than to raise our consciousness about the process?

What About Destructive Spirits?

The positive goal of consciousness-raising to learn about spirituality and one's life purpose aside, I must include a strong word of caution with regard to ghostly communication. Using a ouija board or automatic writing as a game and then communicating with whomever shows up is flirting with danger. Even if the energy identifies itself as someone familiar, there is no guarantee that they are who they claim to be. They may seem playful to you while in actuality they are seeking an anchor by which to remain connected to the physical world.

What motive might a spirit have for such an act? Motives are many and varied—one example of a spirit with a motive to mislead you is a deceased drug addict. Mediums believe that those who die while addicted to drugs often return, seeking a host body in which to satisfy their chemical craving. Such a scenario reflects what possession and obsession is all about.

If you have attracted an unfamiliar or negative energy, you will know it. It is, in general, not a pleasant sensation. You might feel invaded or, at the least, very uncomfortable. People often report a musty smell or a moaning sound during such a time. Sometimes a cold, clammy feeling accompanies a negative or unhealthy presence. Always be prepared by surrounding yourself in a protective shell of white light when you open yourself to the spirit world. Also, don't hesitate to call on your spirit guides or guardian angels for assistance in the event that you sense a negative energy in your vicinity.

Exorcising an Aggressive Spirit

While at a bed and breakfast in the Gold Country on one of the picturesque back roads of California, Shirl and I encountered a big-time negative energy force. We had been attending a marriage ceremony at the inn when we heard that during the course of the previous evening, two guests had separately encountered what appeared to be the same ghost.

When Shirl and I asked the proprietor if there was a resident spirit, he confirmed that not only had numerous guests reported seeing it, but that the encounters were generally uncannily identical. It was almost always perceived as a woman who looked like a dance hall hostess wearing a long dress and a large hat. She did not appear to be menacing, and the guests were often more amused than fearful.

When the owner of the inn learned that I was a psychic, he assumed a more serious tone.

"You know, we have a separate, smaller, two-story house behind the rear garden area that we use for overflow guests. Have you walked over there?" he asked quietly, looking around to ensure that he was not being overheard.

I shook my head no.

"Well, I think we have another one in that house—only it's a bit more . . . ahhh . . . threatening."

"Threatening?"

"Say, how would you like stay in the rear house as my guest so that you can tell me what's *really* going on?" he asked in an upbeat mode. "It's not used that much, but there have been strange things going on back there."

"*Threatening?*" I asked again.

He paused and thought. "Well, he's not threatening to *everyone*—just the ones he doesn't like."

If his last statement was to meant to provide additional comfort, it missed the mark entirely.

The owner went on to relay the whole story. Recently a couple had been occupying a room on the second floor of the rear house and the man claimed he was jostled by something he couldn't see. It had been reported by other guests that he had been yelling and pushing his girlfriend around in his room when he was suddenly lifted into the air and thrown into the hallway. Then he was pushed down the stairs. There were several witnesses corroborating his story and the police were even called in to investigate.

"Many folks have stayed there without incident, of course, but I would sure like to know what's going on," he said nervously. His wife, who had appeared at his side during the telling of the story, nodded her head in confirmation.

And then he added as if an afterthought, "—because this is the *second* time this spirit has acted violently."

"Oh boy, another adventure!" chimed in my wife, who had been listening to our conversation.

After walking through the rear house and checking with a few guests who had slept there without incident the previous evening, we agreed to return another evening with the intention of instructing this energy to leave. If a ghost haunts a specific location, it is usually because it feels attracted to it for some reason originating in the spirit's physical life. Often all one has to do is convince the energy that it is now in spirit form and no longer has a purpose in the physical world.

I am aware of instances where innocent people have been possessed by a ghostly spirit—but I reasoned that if we protected ourselves properly, we would be safe. Shirl, of course, was delighted by the challenge.

We returned several months later and stayed overnight, well-armed with a bag of our metaphysical tools. Upon our arrival, we immediately cleansed the house thoroughly with our favorite crystals, freshly cut sage and a few Native American ceremonies we had carefully researched.

We spent the night in the same room where the previous ghostly encounters had occurred. The evening was mostly peaceful and without incident—if you discount the three or four terrifying hours we remained wide awake, listening to assorted muffled noises and unidentifiable sounds of movement originating from the corridor just outside the walls of our room!

Early the next morning, we created a ceremony in the hallway where we had heard the noises the previous night. This was the spot where both pushing incidents were said to have occurred. We placed our crystals in a circle around us, invoked the loving light of protection, and invited the ghost to move from the premises. We asked him to understand that his business here was complete and that it was time to leave this earth plane and advance to the God light.

We brought the procedure to completion when we sensed our message had been received. We felt an increased peaceful feeling and surmised that the negative energy had departed.

Then suddenly, without warning, we heard a thunderous bang!

We sat there frozen, half scared out of our wits. I turned around and saw that one end of a large, concealed, retractable metal stairway had dropped from the ceiling to the hall floor, not more than twenty feet away from where we were sitting. My mind immediately flashed back to those early 1950s movies, the ones with the phony looking amphibian-like aliens descending a ladder from a saucer-shaped spacecraft hovering above.

Our spirit may have departed—but he sure had the final word!

chapter 14

A Haunted Mansion

IN ORDER TO extricate a bothersome ghost from a physical environment, it is helpful to first determine *why* it has remained connected to the corporeal world. When Shirl's father appeared to us shortly after he died, it was to deliver a message. Once the communication was received, her dad's energy quickly dissipated, never to return—unless you count the intermittent blinking of household lights each year on or near the anniversary of his death.

Ten years ago, when Shirl and I encountered the ghost of a young boy in a German castle, he announced that he had been wreaking havoc because the bed where he had been murdered was removed from his room. Once the bed was replaced to his satisfaction, he immediately ceased to be disruptive.

The ghosts we discovered in a trendy pub in the Tyburn Village area of London continue to reside there because of the suffering they experienced nearly *two centuries* ago. The basement of the building had been a torture chamber for political prisoners, after which they were hung by the neck on a gallows in the adjacent public square. Despite our efforts to remove these ghosts, they remained such an angry and powerful collective energy that they continue, to this day, to break or damage anything stored in the cellar when the doors to what were their cells are closed. Sadly, because they were so brutally murdered, I question whether they will ever be able to find peace.

Electrical disturbances are often commonplace when spirits are present. Photographers have captured inexplicable images where ghosts have been sensed or observed. People attending séances have reported a flashes-of-light phenomenon when residents of the ethereal world are summoned. Electrical disturbances result from the ghostly energies' arrival, and might be equated to a bolt of lightning occurring when two differing atmospheric conditions meet head-on.

The Truth about Ghosts

A common misconception about ghosts is that they typically haunt old, medieval creaky castles or hang around ancient battlefields flashing lights, making odd noises, and brandishing chains. Many people assume that these entities have returned from some ghostly graveyard seeking vengeance following a brutal murder or a sworn deathbed curse. Poltergeist activity, such as objects that move without a natural explanation, is often assumed to be an attempt on the part of a ghostly entity to inspire fright. We may even think of such tactics by a ghost as a method of scaring a baneful and immoral individual who has evil in his heart—possibly to even some sort of score.

If ghosts were all righteous murdered souls attached to the place where they were mistreated or killed, how could one explain paranormal disturbances in the relatively *new* home of a well-respected and prominent surgeon in an exclusive Northern California suburb?

The Way Home

A sympathetic mutual friend gave the physician my name and Shirl's, anticipating that we might be able to explain the strange phenomenon occurring in his home with increasing frequency. When we spoke by telephone, the doctor said that although he didn't believe in ghosts, *something* was going on his house and this mysterious something was causing anxiety for his entire family. His wife and daughters had relocated to their summer home because of the disturbances—he wondered if we could come out and "do something."

As he elaborated, I learned that when he set foot in his living room, a wall-mounted windup clock would stop. This would only occur when *he* entered the room—usually when he was alone. He reported that the built-in vacuum system in the house, the television set, and the power tools in his garage were frequently turning on by themselves when he returned home after a difficult and exhausting day of surgery. He cited numerous additional examples of equally inexplicable occurrences, each seemingly hinging on *his* personal activities, and each similarly perplexing. He finished by stating that he had even employed numerous electronic and electrical technicians to investigate the problem without any success.

I told him that it sounded to me like the incidents could be a result of some sort of poltergeist or ghostly activity, and said that although we couldn't promise anything, my wife and I would be willing to give him our thoughts. When did he want us to come out?

His immediate reply, "How about this afternoon?" indicated the seriousness of his concern.

The doctor left our name at the gate of the fortress community where he resided, and a skeptical security guard promptly and efficiently directed us to the his house. It was a huge residence, perched on the side of a hill in a pristine neighborhood at the end of a wide cul-de-sac. The well-manicured gardens and the numerous walkway signs warning of an elaborate alarm system was a good indication that vandals or mischief-makers were probably not the culprit.

Greeting us at the door, he cautiously invited us in. He reiterated that we wouldn't be disturbed since his wife and two daughters had left town due to the increased tempo of the spooky occurrences. His entire manner suggested that, as a person of intelligent genetic stock who was obviously well-educated and a respected pillar of the medical community, he was uncomfortable even considering whatever weird things we might want to do.

As he slowly led us through the numerous and well-furnished rooms, Shirl and I individually sensed that the uncomfortable something was confined to one specific area of the two-story house. We could feel its heavy negative energy. It felt like we were intruding in its space. I'm sure you know what I mean—we can all sense these ponderous feelings in one form or another, at one time or another.

Have you ever suspected that something is wrong or out of place, but are unable to put your finger on it? Or that you must check on a small child only to discover that they need your help? In the doctor's home, the "knowing" was a disquieting feeling . . . like something didn't belong. Even though I had never been in the house before, I could clearly sense that a foreign energy was intruding on the life of this family. There was nothing to see and nothing to hear that supported my conclusion—but the feeling was irrefutable. I just knew.

After exploring the house, we discovered that we felt most uncomfortable in the master bedroom's large, walk-in closet and bathroom. We felt very unwelcome. The doctor seemed to be a little on edge in this area and Shirl made a quick exit under the illogical pretense of wishing to examine another room.

"This is the area of the greatest negative intensity," I said softly. "Isn't the living room—and the clock—beneath this part of the house?"

The expression on his face told me that I was correct.

"How about stepping out of the room for a moment?" I asked the extremely nervous doctor. I had no idea what I would do next and thought my guides might give some greatly needed insight.

The doctor didn't have to be asked a second time.

I sat down on the floor of the bedroom and waited for direction. Since channelers seldom actually "hear" anything, I expected that I would "know" what action I was to follow by tuning into the pipeline from which my information flows. This was the same process that I use when I read psychically for clients: I just get in their "space," open my mouth and verbalize the words that are there.

I also liken it to reciting a childhood nursery rhyme I learned as a little boy and have repeated to my children and grandchildren so many times that I am not even consciously aware of what the words mean anymore. The sounds are just extracted from some sort of holding or storage place where they reside until summoned.

Have you ever done something so many times that you no longer pay attention to the process of doing it? Being psychic is much like that. It is a near-hypnotic state during which involuntary reflexes seem to determine what to do or say. When I encountered Shirl's father six months after he died, I just let him speak through me. It was the same with the ghost in the German castle. I realized that the message here was to trust the same procedure—to stick with what worked.

Soon, I was inclined to act. I summoned my wife and the doctor, motioning for them to sit on the floor by me near the master bedroom closet. I took the crystals that we'd brought and deposited them in the center of our circle of three. I quieted myself in meditation, preparing to channel what was to come. Shirl, on the other hand, felt a need to satisfy her urge to minutely adjust the position of each of the psychic stones I had set in place. The doctor, observing the two of us busily completing our tasks, squirmed nervously.

So here we were, Shirl and I—two middle-aged, new-age metaphysicians—hunkered down on the floor in the bedroom of an exclusive suburban mansion. We were doing our metaphysical thing, joined by an extremely uncomfortable owner, still attired in his very stylish and expensive business suit, clearly wishing he were someplace else.

"It's a young boy," I heard myself whisper even before I realized I had made a sound. "It's the ghost of a young boy who has recently died and has attached himself to you." The doctor's expression told me he thought he knew the boy to whom I was referring.

"When did the strange events begin to occur?" I asked. The look changed to unmistakable confirmation.

"When he died," the doctor said softly. He relayed an emotional story involving an emergency room surgery on a young boy following a terrible auto accident. The child's mother and dad had died in the crash but the young boy's life was saved under the doctor's skillful care. Visiting the boy daily during his slow convalescence, the doctor grew quite attached to the child—becoming, in effect, a substitute parent. Then, unexpectedly, the boy died.

"That's when the ghostly activity began?" Shirl asked gently.

He nodded his head as he wiped a single tear from his cheek. We continued to sit in the circle while Shirl and I informed the spirit of the young boy that it was time for him to leave the house.

"Go to the light," we repeated over and over.

We advised him to look for his parents in the tunnel. We then performed a few simple ceremonies, smudged the room a bit, and invoked the power of the crystals.

Loving thoughts often counter the fear and the subsequent confusion that detains a ghostly energy from moving on. It is no different in physical life. When you let go of fear, you will begin to perceive what has always been there. As you expand your awareness, you see things you just haven't noticed before.

When we completed our ritual, the doctor shared a few personal thoughts from his heart. As we listened to his feelings, it became apparent why the boy's energy had attached itself to the doctor. Having lost his entire family in the accident, the child had become terrified. Confused by his ordeal and suddenly all alone, the young soul had attached himself to the only person on the physical plane to whom he felt a connection.

As the feeling in the room gradually lightened, we knew that the "boy" was on his way home.

Love sometimes requires us to let go.

chapter 15

The **Importance** of **Proper Closure**

NOW THAT WE have discussed how to open to our inherent psychic and spiritual nature, we need to acquire the ability to close down the connection when we are finished—a concept all too often overlooked. We must always remember to disengage—to shut down our psychic pores when we return from the metaphysical world.

When we enter the realm of spirit, our bodies are often left vulnerable to the non-physical negative energy that lingers about as though waiting for a host. Many indigenous tribal shamans believe that diseases result from our susceptibility to this wayward force. Our physical being is left unguarded and defenseless when a portion of our consciousness leaves for an extended period of time. The same thing happens when we neglect to close our psychic centers upon our return to normal consciousness. Closure is particularly necessary when we are preparing to do something potentially dangerous, such as drive a car, complete our income tax return . . . or lend money to in-laws.

Think about it. Religious celebrations always include some sort of proper closure. A Christian church service culminates with a benediction—a completion of the liturgy and also an administration of spiritual protection. Even my son's Indian Guides[1] ceremony had a means of termination: *May the great spirit of all great spirits be with you now and forever more.* Yet, after meditation or connection with our spirit guides, we often jump back into the physical world without properly signing off.

When I first began my metaphysical work, I did not realize the importance of closure following a channeling session. I remember meeting some friends at a restaurant one evening following a psychic reading and was emotionally upbeat, looking forward to the evening. As soon as we were seated at a table, I inexplicably began to feel angry. As the evening rolled on, I became increasing hostile but couldn't understand the sudden shift in my mood. Finally, an emotional outburst at a nearby table made me realize that I had been sensing and absorbing *someone else's* feelings, not my own.

Another potential problem with incomplete closure is the resultant feeling of being spacy or disjointed. This occurs when a part of our awareness remains in the spiritual realm. As we attempt to return to normal activities we may feel ungrounded—like a fish out of water. We might feel, do, or say things that we would not otherwise consider if our normal, socially attuned control mechanisms were firmly in place.

---

1. An organization not unlike the Cub Scouts, except that fathers are *required* to accompany their sons to Indian Guides events.

The **Importance** of **Balance**

A short-term visit to the spiritual world can be very user friendly. However, too much time spent in this domain can be disorienting. Those who journey out-of-body (OBE) may report their limited-time experience as desirable, but they will often require reassurance that their spiritual body's "silver cord" is firmly connected to their physical body.[2] Frequently, first time OBE voyagers fear that they might float away or become lost. Not unlike an umbilical chord, the silver cord serves as a tether—a way back.

When I first opened to my psychic ability, I became so excited about the plethora of opportunities to use my newly discovered talent that I constantly remained connected to this supersensory space. Possessing the potential to know what others were thinking or what was going to occur in the future was a powerful feeling. However, as I would venture into large crowds, I would begin to feel uncomfortable, suffer headaches or become despondent and depressed. I soon realized that I was picking up the "waste" of those around me. Negative energy has a way of spreading, just as germs do when someone with a cold sneezes. In addition to absorbing the emotions of strangers, I became easily disoriented and had a hard time discriminating my own thoughts and feelings from those of the people around me. My strong advice, again, is to close down whatever doorways you have opened when you reenter the everyday world of physical reality.

How to Achieve Closure

When I prepare myself for a psychic reading, I often visualize a portal in my body in the region of my third eye and crown chakras. I visualize a crystal cave above my head, then raise my conscious

---

2. During an out-of-body experience, the voyager's consciousness leaves the physical body, traveling in the astral (or subtle) body. Those who have had this experience often report that they remain connected to their physical body by a silver cord, which ensures that the astral and physical bodies will be reunited and consciousness restored to the physical body. Purposeful travels out-of-body are referred to as *astral projection*—some practitioners of this method believe that if the silver cord is severed, the discarnate consciousness may become lost.

attention into the glittering space. By implementing a destination for my consciousness during my altered states, I can easily close down my connection by visualizing my consciousness *returning* from that "place" and reentering normal consciousness. When I have completed my work, I can easily return my consciousness to my body through the portal I have created, close the psychic opening that I have visualized and utilized, and "downsize" the expanded consciousness or energy light circle that I have expanded around my body.

I secure the psychic doorway I have opened just as I might lock my residence when leaving for a period of time—drawing in the perimeter fence and filling my moat with protective water.

When you retract the love light you expanded from your heart chakra into a tight-fitting envelope around your body, you are protecting yourself from negative psychic penetration. I always instruct my clients to expand their light before I begin a psychic reading and inform them that Sami, my channeling guide, will be poking around in their light space. I also remind them that, at the conclusion of the reading, they must pull their light in close to their body. Not unlike a fortress, as we pull our walls in they become stronger, more dense, and more difficult to penetrate by negative external forces.

This process is useful when you need your own private space or you fear being intruded upon by others. When we covet privacy with our thoughts, don't we generally go off by ourselves, withdrawing from all others? Likewise, we can eliminate the distractions of the outside world by closing down the energy circle so that we are shielded from the psychic influence of others.

People who are reaching out emotionally can often psychically tap into our energy without intending to harm us. They can even drain our life force if we are not on guard. On the other hand, when we want to be loved and appreciated, we expand our light. When we want to be held, we open our arms and bring our loved ones near our heart. When we desire to be heard, we reach out with our light to bring others into our psychic or emotional space.

Keeping in Touch with Your Guides

When we return from a state of higher consciousness, properly close our psychic channels, and lock the door, you might be wondering: How can we communicate with our spirit guides? How will we know if they want to get in touch with us? The answer is simple: by implementing closure, we are *not* blocking incoming messages from our guidance. Not at all. Once we establish our spirit-guided communication system, the spiritual phone will ring when someone is on the line. Closing down only prevents distracting static or a negative obscene phone call; it's a means to protect yourself from unnecessary spiritual fodder. And once we learn how to establish the connection with our guides, we become a permanent subscriber.

As you access the spirit world with greater frequency, you will be able to open and close your energy field with increasing ease. It will eventually become an automatic reflex requiring little thought.

How to Screen Incoming Messages

One of the difficulties encountered when beginning to open to your psychic self is determining the *source* of your ideas and inspirations. Did the thought originate from your higher spiritual guidance? Is it your inner secret desire? Or was it, perhaps, telepathically "borrowed" from someone else? Remember, when you receive information using your psychic senses, you *are* tapping into the truth . . . it just may not be yours!

Being telepathic has great value and affords great potential. It is also an easy skill to abuse if you remain ignorant about your boundaries. If you intrusively read another's thoughts and claim them as yours, the karma god may record a negative debit on your account. So how can you determine what's yours and what's not?

The first step is to determine if you are telepathic. Give yourself the following tests:

1. Observe whether you tend to know what others are thinking. Ask yourself: Do I begin many of my sentences with *I knew you were going to say that . . . ?*

2. Locate a deck of playing cards and have your partner project red or black as he or she concentrates on the colors. Ask yourself: Did I have strong feelings about the ones I got right? This might also indicate that you are precognating (knowing what is going to happen in the future). However, if it is most accurate when you are in a crowd or near people with whom you are comfortable, it is likely that you are, indeed, telepathic.

Once you are certain that you *are* telepathic, and therefore able to pick others' messages up either intentionally or accidentally, how can you determine whether the information that you are receiving is meant for you or for another? Is it *your* truth or not? The answer is simple: instruct your guides to assist you.

The Keys to Determining a Message Is for You

1. Before you act on your thought, ask your higher self if it is in your best interest to follow a particular course of action, and then follow your feelings.

2. Remember that the flow of energy is a two-way street. If you avoid projecting negative thought or energy onto someone else, you will be less susceptible to the energy of others. In like manner, if you avoid thrusting what you perceive as your truth on all those around you, you will be less affected by the influence of others' perceived truth on you. What goes around comes around.

3. Pay attention to your body. Notice how and where you react when you begin to get what you know are genuinely *your* feelings. Do you perceive your truth in your gut, do you comprehend it through your third eye, or does your heart know that the message is genuine?

4. Pay attention to your feelings. Ask yourself how you feel about the information that you receive. Begin to associate different feelings with the thoughts or inspirations you know to be yours as compared to moments when you seem to be receptive to the feelings of others.

5. Utilize the protective shell of white light during any correspondence with your spirit guides. Also, be sure that it is retracted and in place when you return to normal consciousness. If you surround yourself with the white light of love expanded from your inner self, you will be less likely to receive information that is detrimental to your well-being.

6. Begin to recognize where and when you are most receptive to your truth—your knowing. Keep a journal, recording when your hunches and feelings are most accurate. Observe your emotions, the time of day, and what is happening in the space around you when you receive the clearest psychic "hits." Are you more receptive with your guidance when you are at work or at play? Are you most connected when you are under pressure and require a quick and accurate response or when you are relaxed and daydreaming? Are you receiving the most accurate impressions first thing in the morning, upon waking, or is it later in the evening when your defenses are down? Do you tend to "see" things or "hear" answers?

The Truth Is Out There

If the thoughts that you receive are yours, you *will* begin to recognize them as your truth . . . regardless of the source. Each of us possesses an individual set of truths: I love this vegetable . . . that sound is very soothing . . . that idea doesn't work for me . . . this place makes me uncomfortable. Your discernment of *your* truth may be different than another person's. After all, truth is rarely universal. In the end, each of us has our own reality, and our realities differ. As they say, beauty is in the eye of the beholder.

Your truth is out there. All you need to do is trust your guides to bring it to you. You selected them before this life and you asked them to assist you—let them do it.

Oh . . . and your mom wanted me to remind you not to forget to say *thank you* . . . .

chapter 16

In Search of Missing Persons

BEING PSYCHIC DOES have its drawbacks. The good news is that you are *psychic* and as a result have access to spiritual information. The bad news is that you *are* psychic and you can't always pick and choose the information you're going to receive.

Late one evening, I received a disturbing telephone call from a very good friend.

"My daughter's gone . . ." said the shaky voice on the other end of the line.

You can have one of ours was my flippant first thought, probably put there by Amy, my light-hearted spirit guide. Fortunately, Joel (the straight, pensive one with the socks

133

that don't always match) suggested that I keep my inappropriate retort to myself.

"Gone?" was my more mature response.

"My daughter and a few of her close friends were walking along the coastline cliffs overlooking the ocean. When they stopped to regroup, she wasn't there."

Between sobs, she relayed the full story. Her daughter Kim and a few school chums were on a nature walk, climbing along a rocky coastline trail overlooking the Pacific Ocean. One of her girlfriends on the hike said that Kim had been in front of her and had stopped to let her go past. When she reached the other side of the ridge that they were climbing, she turned and waited . . . but Kim never appeared. Although her friends went back to look for her, she was nowhere to be found.

"Can you help me?" came the desperate plea. "Is she all right?"

It's a question no psychic *ever* wants to hear from a friend.

Being psychic is usually a desirable and rewarding experience. The wonderful glow that remains following a successful psychic reading with a total stranger is difficult to express. Even when I speak in front of a predominately male, left-brained, closed-minded professional service club meeting, for example, and less than fifty percent look like they would rather be somewhere else, I feel like I've been successful.

However, when a psychic receives a call like this from someone close to them and they know they may not be able to deliver the news the client desperately wants to hear, it's not easy—and the glow of an accurate reading is diminished (to say the least) if the news turns out to be bad.

You want so much to provide comforting words and assistance to your friend that it can be easy to lose your objectivity. You desperately hope that what comes through are only positive words, because you don't know if you can deliver the other kind. Naturally, when you read for someone about whom you have strong feelings, you are emotionally invested in the outcome. This is the reason doctors never operate on members of their own family. Although they desire only the best for each one of their patients, the fervent feeling involved with potential harm to a close loved one can easily cloud their objectivity.

Reading for a Victim

Anytime you're dealing with a potential victim, the reading can be difficult. With an audience of highly emotionally involved people who want only the best news from you, the pressure is great to perform. But even working with law enforcement agencies on cases about potential victims of criminal activity is easier than responding to *Is my daughter okay?* when asked by a dear friend.

The police are typically a close-minded bunch who only call you when they're truly stumped. I think they secretly want to be able to tell the press that they've done everything they could . . . left no stone unturned . . . followed every lead. You can almost hear the final press release: "—and we even called in one of those weird psychic fortune tellers . . . ."

A Kidnapping for Christmas

I recently worked on a kidnapping case in a Northern California suburb the week before Christmas. In this case, I was summoned by the family, not the police. I remember walking past the yellow-taped crime scene boundaries and the press corps only to be turned away at the door by a uniformed law enforcement officer who scoffed when I told him who I was and why I was there.

The family, more desperately concerned with whether their mom was okay than catching the bad guys, found and sequestered me in an adjacent room. I sat on the missing woman's bed and, in an attempt to feel her presence, held several of her objects. I concluded that she was in good health and was bound and blindfolded in a garage not far from where we sat. I reported that she would be released on Christmas Day at some distance from where she was being held. Although I was informed that her husband owned a jewelry store, I felt she would be released before any ransom was requested or paid.

"They haven't asked for any money yet," responded one of the daughters. "The police say they're waiting for the call."

I went on to share the general rural location where I felt she was being restrained.

"She's unhurt," I repeated, and assured the concerned children that it was going to be a relatively short ordeal.

It was quite an experience to be sitting on the bed of a woman I had never met with a zillion policepersons in the outer room and a crowd of curious onlookers, camera trucks with satellite dishes, and reporters surrounding the house. The police had no interest in what I said and the family was too scared to know if they should believe me. After I relayed all the information Sami had provided, I was given a pleasant "Thanks for coming . . ." and scooted out the door.

Thankfully, it turned out that my information was correct. She had been tied up and blindfolded in a garage. She had not been harmed and was subsequently released (without any payment being asked for or made) in a suburban town some distance from where she had been held. I got the day wrong, though—she was released on Christmas *Eve*.

Difficult as an emotion-filled incident like this may have been, the fact remains that reading for people you don't know and telling them things they want to hear is quite different than having to face a friend who has posed the dreaded question: *Is my daughter okay?*

The Search for Kim

I suggested to my friend whose daughter was missing that I needed a little time with her question and that I would call her back when I had something to report. I went into the room I use for my psychic readings and closed the door. I only knew Kim superficially, which was an advantage in a situation like this, considering the emotion that was packed around her mom's inquiry.

I followed my normal procedure as closely as possible and cleared my mind in order to make space for Sami's answer. Suddenly, I began to feel like I was floating—I had to open my eyes to ensure that I had not begun to levitate. I hadn't. I felt very much at peace. It was as though I were being held by an angel in an aura of love.

After receiving little more than this, I called my friend back to suggest that I was getting very little psychic information. Although I could not get a fix on her location, I was certain her daughter was not uncomfortable because I was in touch with her feelings and she was very much at peace.

Muffled sobbing from the other end of the telephone suggested that my friend understood what I was attempting to avoid articulating. Needing to fill the awkward silence, I mumbled something to the effect that I knew she was not in physical danger, hadn't been kidnapped, and was not in any pain.

"She died, didn't she?"

"I don't know that," I quickly responded, wishing I could provide greater reassurance. I finished by saying, "I do have the feeling that she will contact you tomorrow by mid-morning."

"You're telling me that she died," my friend said quietly. She thanked me and then gently hung up. Several days later the police closed the case as an accidental drowning.

That was one of the toughest assignments I ever faced.

But you know, there were major lessons learned by all the participants in this scenario. Kim's leaving was not one of those random acts of fate. It wasn't the Fate Guy fooling around, as my friend Ron is fond of saying.

Karma was being acted out and completed here and each person touched by this experience grew spiritually in the process. Who are we to attempt to fathom the subtle workings of the universe or to comprehend purpose in personal tragedies orchestrated by the Creator Force?

All we can do is play our small role in the greater drama.

All we can do is to gain value from the experiences we each create.

Oh . . . and the part about my friend being contacted by her daughter the next day following our conversation? She later confided to me that she had been sitting in her kitchen the morning after her daughter's disappearance, exhausted by the long vigil she had maintained throughout the night. Suddenly her daughter appeared in front of her. Kim smiled and reached out to her mom's heart. My friend said her grief dissipated for just a moment and she felt an incredible sense of peace. She said she had no idea of the length of time she maintained this vision, but she swears she was not asleep and it was not just a dream.

Kim had returned to communicate that she was all right.

chapter 17

The Search for Missing Objects

WE ALL KNOW the old expression "Change your viewpoint and you change your reality." Well, it's time to add another line: Change the viewpoint of *others* and you change your reality—as well as theirs.

Take the following example: A newspaper woman from a Northern California magazine had contacted me to set up an interview pertaining to my first book. To say that she was "less than enthusiastic" about the topic of her assignment might best describe her preconditioned mindset. She was a card-carrying skeptic, and as you might expect, such a scenario doesn't make for the best psychic performances.

The opening sentences of the article, which eventually appeared in the periodical, read:

> *When it comes to the supernatural, I am a reluctant*
> *believer. But the new age airy-fairyness that spreads*
> *in California as rampantly as eucalyptus trees gives*
> *me the willies.*[1]

Not exactly one of my metaphysical groupies . . . .

In spite of the reporter's resistance, the interview progressed fairly well. During a mini-reading following our Q-and-A session, I had actually been able to penetrate her skeptical point of view regarding psychic phenomenon by accurately pinpointing specifics about her husband, parents, childhood, and a few key events in her life. Although she revealed little as she left our house, I was confident that the published article would turn out favorably if only she were able to remain objective.

Several days later she telephoned me and inquired if she had left her reading glasses at my house. I responded that I didn't think she had, but I would search for them and would notify her if they turned up.

She called me again the following day and asked if I had located them yet. I informed her that I had retraced her steps and looked under and behind every likely place they could've been hiding—glasses seem to like to do that, you know—but they were not to be found.

"Well, if you're as good a psychic as you claim to be, how about locating them for me?" she said boldly.

You don't have to be psychic to know that the tone of the article probably depended on my response to her inquiry. Unfortunately, a seer is often perceived to be as good as his or her last reading—so whatever I told her had to be right on or the final draft would likely reflect her negative personal prejudice.

---

1. "Psyched Out." Excerpted with permission from *Diablo Magazine*. Walnut Creek, CA: Diablo Publications, November 1995.

The **Nature** of **Psychic Awareness**

Most people are not aware that psychics do not magically "see" answers. At least this psychic doesn't. Being clairvoyant does not provide an instantaneous private viewing of a movie-like vision on a large theater screen. There are no rewind or playback features such as you would find on a VCR. Since psychics work most effectively when removed from emotional pressure, the reporter's request would not be an easy assignment. She was challenging me to prove my authenticity. To complicate matters, the results were more likely to be favorable if I could be in her physical energy field rather than being distanced by a phone line.

Doing a reading when being challenged by a skeptic who expects you to fail in order to validate their own personal belief system makes the process much more difficult. The pressure is particularly oppressive if you happen to be working in front of a large group of people, for instance on television. Psychics are expected to be 100 percent accurate while adhering to time restraints in front of an often skeptical audience.

Uri Geller, a well-known and authentic psychic, was deemed to have used trickery when attempting to psychically bend a spoon on cue during an interview on *The Tonight Show* with Johnny Carson. Unfortunately, this practitioner succumbed to the pressure of the challenge he was presented with: to prove his psychic ability in a negative and restrictive environment. He resorted to deception, and his reputation was ruined—all because of a direct confrontation to his pride and ego.

With my newspaper interviewer waiting for an answer, I hastily called on my guide Sami for a quick consultation. I did not dare involve my more playful guide, Amy, for fear of what she might say.

"Well . . . ?" came the impatient voice on the telephone.

I opened my mouth and heard myself say, "It's no accident that you have misplaced your glasses. You will now be given the opportunity to learn how to activate your psychic gift in order to find them."

"Oh?" she said with somewhat less enthusiasm.

I informed her that her guides would assist her in finding them.

"Look in a place you've already searched thoroughly," I stated, as per Sami's insistence.

Quoting the last three paragraphs of her article:

> Who knows why, but I go straight to my car and feel under my car seat—the very same place I had scoured the day before. Presto: my glasses. I call Coburn back.
>
> "There are two explanations," he says. "One, you just hadn't looked hard enough the first time. Two, your spiritual guide knew you were going to look there and manifested them for you."
>
> "Well, that's a little hard to believe," I say.
>
> "Whether you believe it or not doesn't matter," he says. "At least you have your glasses back!"

I think there were several lessons here. First, sometimes we learn best when forced to move off a hard and fixed position.

And second, when you get what you want, don't get stuck in the details regarding *how* you got it. In the wise words of an anonymous philosopher, "Who cares what the postman looks like—as long as he delivers the check!"

How to Enhance Your Reception

So—how do you go about being your own psychic? My first answer is, of course, to make contact with your spirit guides and ask them for assistance. If you've had trouble connecting with your guidance or haven't yet accepted the presence of these unseen spiritual forms, then begin by simply expanding your awareness. For example, as your eyes focus on this page, broaden your peripheral vision to other objects in your immediate vicinity. Become aware of other people or objects in your environment . . . the routine noises you haven't previously noticed . . . and the primary colors around you. Expand the radius of your energy as though you are reaching out for something just beyond your grasp.

Remember, *everything* is energy—and because all energy vibrates, you can tune in to this vibration as you would the frequency of a radio station. Our collective life experiences have programmed us to ignore extraneous information that might distract us from the object of our immediate focus. If we're driving a car, for instance, we generally concentrate on only the tasks that require our attention. We've learned to tune out the bombardment of nonessential external stimuli.

You now have a new assignment: *Learn to tune it in.*

Being in tune with psychic or intuitive impressions is about letting go of the doubts and limiting belief systems and trusting your inner senses—your feelings. On a subconscious level, we do this all the time, don't we? If you are setting the dining room table for a formal dinner party, isn't it your inner feeling that directs the placement of the flower arrangement? When you are getting dressed for an important evening out, don't you wear what "feels" right?

These kinds of decisions are generally not deduced through logic and sound reasoning. They are an aspect or your emotional nature—your feelings. Some people might be more sensitive to an inner voice telling them what to do; others may picture the results in their imagination or mind's eye. A few might claim to just know.

Pay attention to *how* you sense things around you. When you say to yourself, *I knew that was going to happen*, what sense told you so?

The Practice of Finding

If you wish to utilize your newly developed sixth sense to psychically ascertain the outcome or resolution of something, or to find a missing object, follow these simple guidelines:

1. Make a heart connection with the object or person you wish to find or "read." In the case of the woman with the lost glasses, I began by making an emotional bond with her, as if I were looking through her eyes and feeling her feelings.

2. Listen to your spirit guides. They will assist you by providing clues such as a word, a mental picture or intuitive knowing.

3. Look around your environment for signs—you may notice something out of place or be presented with a synchronistic "coincidence."

Having done this for so long, it's probably much easier for me to trust the impressions that I receive—but all it takes for you to succeed is a little patience and the expectation that you *can* do it.

However, be aware that we tend to lose our objectivity when we are emotionally involved in the outcome. I'm the last person to be able to find *my* stuff when it has been misplaced. If I'm pressured to find something like my own car keys in a narrow time frame, I may as well forget it. If I wish to know how my workshop will be received or what the results of a football game that I have fifty dollars riding on will be, I'm guessing like everyone else. But place me at the crap table without any money invested and I can often be as accurate as a prophet.

I would advise you to first relax and let go of the frustration you might be experiencing. Some psychics suggest that it is best if you physically remove yourself from the environment involving the issue that needs psychic resolution. Others would advise you to place yourself as close as you can to the proximity of the people or issue on which you are working. Each of us is different. You have to experiment to see what works for you.

Putting It to the Test

"Chuck, this is Sandy—I need your help," said a pleading, half-sobbing female voice on the other end of the telephone.

Sandy, whom I have known for over thirty years, is the wife of one of my regular poker-playing buddies and a real character. The fact that one of her eyes is blue and the other brown speaks to the upbeat, fun role she has signed up to play in this incarnation.

"What's wrong?" I asked.

"I can't find my jewelry . . . do you know where it is?"

"Sandy, I haven't taken your jewelry," I retorted playfully, never knowing in all the years we've been friends just where our lighthearted conversations were going to end up.

"No, this is serious," she insisted. "Dick and I took a trip several months ago and I hid my jewelry so that no one would steal it while we were gone. It worked . . . because now I can't find it either. Can you help me?"

At least she didn't ask *Is my daughter all right? . . .* !

Locating a missing object that I've never seen over the telephone is not what I do best—it generally requires sensing the item's forcefield from a great distance. This is radically different from channeling the energy from an individual sitting before me who desires insight into their spiritual karma. The contrast is little understood by those who naively assume that psychics somehow receive answers spoken by unseen mystical voices or printed on bulletin-boards hanging out in the ethers.

Maybe she should call the reporter you taught to manifest her missing reading glasses, Amy, my precocious guide, jokingly suggested before disappearing in an imaginary puff of smoke.

Thanks a lot, I replied silently to my playful spiritual friend.

"Hello—you still there?" Sandy asked. "Can you find them for me?"

"*Them?* You lost more than one piece of jewelry?"

"I told you—" she quickly responded, "I didn't *lose* them, I just . . . don't know where they are! I don't remember where I hid my five-carat diamond ring, a valuable emerald ring, a sapphire ring and an *irreplaceable* antique bracelet."

"Oh . . ." I said quietly. "I can see why you're frantic."

I recalled my mom doing the same thing with my sister Carolyn's jewelry when Carolyn went on an extended vacation some time ago. She brought a bag containing all of her valuables to my mother's house for safekeeping. My mom decided to hide it in a place least likely to be discovered by a burglar. She did a good job because, when my sister returned, neither of them could locate it.

It wasn't until six months later that she found the stuff hidden in an enema bag.

Ask her if she has an enema bag, Amy offered and then quickly left.

"I don't think so . . ." I muttered aloud.

"What?" asked Sandy.

I needed to get focused.

"Okay, Sandy, tell me what you remember."

"I remember hiding my jewelry and now I can't find it. Weren't you listening?" she repeated, impatiently now.

"Okay, okay—let me see what I can do. How long have they been missing? Did you look everywhere? Do you remember which part of the house they're in?" I was attempting to buy a little time while I waited for Sami to get in touch with Sandy's guides. Maybe he was waiting for a dial tone or something.

"They've been missing for three months!"

"Oh . . ." I said again. "Sandy, can I get back to you?"

I went into my reading room to clear my thoughts and meditate. I closed my eyes and attempted to picture her house in my mind's eye. She and Dick had recently moved to a nearby town. I had only been in their new home a few times, most recently at our monthly poker game hosted by Dick several weeks prior.

Knowing Sandy, I assumed that she had not yet confided her dilemma to her husband. I am aware that Dick is a disbeliever in psychic phenomenon because during poker games he comments that if I were really psychic, I would know what cards he's holding. I frequently want to tell him I don't need metaphysical insight when I play poker with him because he always fiddles with his chips when he's bluffing—but I figure that isn't really something he needs to know.

The truth is, of course, that I can only access my psychic gift for the purposes of spiritual enlightenment. I've already told you what happened in Reno. Since my psychic ability is focused on channeling my client's truth, spirit guides seldom reveal whether my poker opponent has successfully filled an inside straight or not. I do have to confess, however, that Bruce—another of my regular poker playing buddies—is not only a good player, but damn lucky! No one else, over the many years, is as lucky as he is and wins as consistently as he does. So, every once in awhile when it's a small pot . . . and it's just he and I in the game . . . and when I am losing and his pile of chips are about ready to topple over . . . I've asked Amy if she'd like to share a little insight. I never receive any *specific* information, of course—but if I hear her laughing, I immediately drop out of the hand.

In any case, back to Sandy's jewelry . . . .

In my meditation, I pictured myself walking down the hall to the back area of her house. My attention was drawn to the master bedroom suite and the large walk-in closet at the far end of the room. Although I was not able to discern the location of her missing rings and bracelet, I was aware that my eyes tended to search areas within a foot or so from the surface of the floor.

Look in the pockets of something old . . . down deep, an unspoken voice seemed to say.

My eyes continued to scan the mental image of her bedroom, but I couldn't pinpoint much beyond the impression that the jewelry resided in the master bedroom and that it had not been stolen.

I called Sandy back. After reminding her that I didn't have a real high batting average with locating missing objects, I shared my conclusions.

"Look in your old clothing—like jackets, coats, and robes. Your jewelry could have slipped through a hole in one of the pockets and ended up in the hem of an old garment."

I added that she might want to search the lower drawers in her dressers and nightstands. I relayed my impression that her precious items might have ended up in a location near the floor, perhaps wrapped up in a seldom-worn item of clothing.

"Good luck," I added.

Later that same afternoon I received a second phone call.

"*I love you!*" blurted Sandy, laughing and chortling in an octave shared only by dog whistles and little girls at slumber parties.

I assumed she had located her rings and bracelet.

"I found them in the pocket of an old bathrobe on the floor in the back corner of my closet!"

I felt a bit of pressure ease from my shoulders. After all, a psychic is only as good as his last accurate hit.

"I don't remember putting them there," she continued. "Anyway, nothing was missing. I'm so relieved—thank you!"

"You can buy me a dinner," I joked. "Or better yet, I'll get Bruce to pay for it."

Bruce, our mutual friend and poker-playing buddy, was also Dick's insurance agent. I figured that Bruce would be greatly relieved not to have to pay out a huge insurance claim.

"Aaaaah . . . maybe you better collect from Dick instead," she said softly.

"Why's that?" I asked.

"Because none of it was insured."

Once developed, you never know when your psychic perception can come in handy. In retrospect, I think Dick owes me more than just one dinner . . . .

chapter 18

Over the Edge of Perception

So—is there a certain type of person who tends to be more psychic than others? Is it a male/female thing? Is age a factor?

Small children are probably the most natural and uninhibited metaphysicians on the planet. They reside comfortably in their own little worlds, which we adults label "make-believe." They are able to readily access their inherent psychic abilities to converse and interact with their imaginary friends or with angels during play time. Parents, of course, generally encourage their offspring to explore their little fantasies . . . that is, as long as they are small children. Once their little ones grow up, adults are quick to teach them that their invisible buddies and the make-believe world are merely figments of the imagination—*not real.*

Society reinforces the distinction between imaginary and real. Most medical professionals, who attend long years of intensive schooling to acquire their impressive credentials, assure us that the imaginary pals of our children are user friendly—the product of a normal childhood. They inform us that the process of pretending provides the little putters the opportunity to enhance their creativity—a tool considered to be beneficial (as long as it's held in check with a good dose of realism and used only in moderate amounts). But the message is consistent: the professionals start to worry if a child doesn't grow out of his or her imaginary world.

We all agree that "children" and "play" go together. Most parents remain confident that their little ones *will* eventually grow out of childhood fantasies and realize that the imaginary world is not compatible with *reality*. As children mature, we assume that they will come to understand a few things: their little friends don't exist, wishing doesn't really work, and Oz is nowhere near Kansas. Or is it?

The **Socialized Reality:**
True or **False?**

As we grow into adulthood, we are schooled in various belief systems designed to reinforce the accepted tenet that intelligence and left-brain logic are considerably more valuable than right-brain intuition and creativity. Public education teaches us that math is an exact science, physics has unwavering rules, and creativity has been deleted due to budget problems. We become so conditioned to this line of reasoning that we actually begin to believe that too much intuition can be dangerous and imagination has little practical value. Can we break the pattern? Of course.

In my experience, women tend to be more psychic than men since women seem to more easily trust and rely on their feelings (another condition of society's determined roles that we were taught as children). However, anyone who is sensitive—of *either* gender—can enhance their psychic abilities with practice.

Those inquisitive individuals who are open to exploring the metaphysical practices of healing and manifestation are encouraged to activate this so-called feminine, or intuitive, part of our consciousness. However, those who have stubbornly determined that this point of view is nonscientific—and therefore invalid—often conclude that the psychic, shaman, or metaphysician resorts to tricks or deception and that any verifiable result of their actions is, at best, a coincidence.

Is that true?

Real Is as Real as Does

A shaman instructing a modern-world apprentice might say, "If you saw, heard it, or felt it, and it *seemed* real, what makes you think it's *not* real? You had a valid experience—it exists in your reality, doesn't it?"

Think about it. Let's say that you "imagine" you hear a tune in your head or you think of a new idea. Is the experience of the tune or idea less valid because it is not in physical form? Because someone else didn't experience it as well? If everyone in the room feels differently than you do about something, does their consensus make *your* feeling less authentic?

From this perspective, we might ask: Just what *are* your child's imaginary friends? Are they just figments of the child's imagination? Or could they possibly be angels or spirit guides? Is it valid or fair to automatically conclude that your child is hallucinating when he or she appears to communicate with them?

There are numerous stories of children who have accurately known about things or events they could not possibly have perceived by way of physical-world reality. When questioned about how they knew, these kids often explained that their imaginary friends informed them. There are countless documented stories about very young children accurately "remembering" events that took place years before their birth. There are youngsters who have recalled specific nuances about places they have never seen or visited . . . at least not in this incarnation. How can we explain their differing view of reality?

Consider the fact that children are recent arrivals on the planet. Might it not be possible that they still possess an impression of a previous lifetime, much as we might remember a past event? If we believe that the human soul is eternal, then it certainly fits with left-brain reasoning that these new arrivals have just descended from the spirit world, and furthermore, that it is information from *that* reality they are recalling.

At the other end of the age spectrum are the elderly. Our dying relatives will often describe viewing an angel or deceased loved one in their presence, seemingly waiting for them. Medical personnel often dismiss such experiences as a hallucinations or suggest that the individual's medication has caused them to become delusional and see or hear things that are not real.

I find it very interesting that those who just arrived on this planet have strikingly similar esoteric experiences as those who are about to return to spirit.

The **Psychic Dream**

Some in our society view dreaming in much the same manner as we perceive a child's fantasy. Dreams are fun to talk about, these people might say, but certainly cannot be taken seriously. They will tell you that nighttime fantasies are products of your imagination, having little value other than to occasionally blow off a little emotional steam. They consider the waking world to be the only consciousness of any value, all else being an elaborate illusion or false reality of some sort. These rationalists will grant you exceptions, of course, such as a psychotherapist's use of dream images to treat a patient. They might concede that a recurring nightmare could provide some insight into understanding the fear or shock resulting from a specific problem— but for the most part it is as useful as puppy poo.

Why does a large segment of our society unquestioningly dismiss the possibility that the dream state is a valid reality? It sure seems real at the time, doesn't it? We wake up kicking and screaming after a terrifying nightmare. We possess an increased sense of fulfillment after having dreamed of a successful conclusion to a lifelong pursuit.

Those who study dreams seriously suggest that, although dreaming might be described as an *altered* state of consciousness, it is a consciousness nevertheless. So—since consciousness is how we experience reality, and dreams are a form of consciousness . . .

Dreams *must* be a form of reality. With that said, the next question might be . . .

Do Dreams Have a Purpose?

Dreams can be many things. They can be informational, containing a taste of ordinary, everyday issues missed in the hectic conscious living of our lives. They can provide insights into problems or concerns following the incubation of a question before sleep. They may serve as an emotional outlet, allowing the dreamer to test problem-solving scenarios, thereby avoiding having to take risks in the waking world. Dreams can provide inspirations for creativity such as ideas for stories, songs, or even inventions. Finally, dreams can be a gateway to the spiritual, psychic, or astral level.

Although some might define all dreaming as a psychic experience, *spiritual-psychic* dreaming is unique. A spiritual-psychic (or lucid) dream is usually characterized by vivid colors and sounds, leaving one with the feeling of having witnessed something strongly ethereal or profound. Intuitively, you sense this kind of dream's importance. You will likely perceive the power of a spiritual-psychic dream and wake up changed by the experience. It's something you won't forget.

Additionally, in a spiritual-psychic dream it is possible for the dreamer to astrally project.[1] You might find that you can visit another dreamer to gain information or solve mutual problems. This process

---

1. Out-of-body experiences are discussed briefly on page 127.

can be far less stressful than it would be in waking consciousness and may allow you to circumvent potentially difficult situations. Karma, too, can be completed in a much less stressful or complicated manner than on the physical plane. You can even confront and face the symbol of your monster or terror and deal with it on this spiritual plane.

In lucid dreams, the dreamer is *aware* that he or she is dreaming, and directs the experience to meet the specific needs of the conscious mind.

Does it really work?

An Evening Visitor

I have a friend who recently had a dream about a mutual friend of ours who lives on the East Coast. He claimed the dream had an extraordinary sense of reality about it—he felt like he had physically visited our friend's apartment. He reported that he was aware of incredible color, sound, and detail that his ordinary dreams lacked. Everything in the dream apartment was the way he remembered it to be, except that all of the furniture in the living room was missing.

I saw my friend again a few days later. He was so intrigued by the intensity of the experience that he had telephoned our mutual acquaintance to share his dream. He learned in the conversation that, on the specific evening of the dream, our friend had removed all the furniture to accommodate the carpet cleaning he had scheduled for the following day. Is it possible that he was actually *there* in some form? In some state of consciousness?

Through the Fabric of Time

Dreams can also be prophetic of the future or recall past-life events. They can function as a warning of an impending event in order to provide your subconscious adequate time to prepare itself. A dream can also be the forerunner for a positive new opportunity that might otherwise be ignored.

Past-life dreams generally involve dramatic, emotional, personal memories and life-altering situations. They will most likely reflect a period setting and are thought to remind us of past-life lessons pertaining to survival or personal growth issues in our current incarnation. These dreams are very common occurrences for children, who might call upon past-life memories to assist them in adapting to their role in this incarnation. These dream-messages reside in the first chakra (survival) and can sometimes be nightmarish. Dreams such as being bitten by a wild animal might prevent the child from teasing an aggressive dog, or falling down a hill in a dream may reign in a young person's otherwise careless behavior.

Spiritual-psychic dreams of this nature can also include strong, emotional past-life events involving others whose energy vibrations are in concert with the dreamer. While in Ecuador, for example, Shirl had a psychic-spiritual dream involving a historical figure associated with the physical environment where we were staying. We had been billeted in an old expansive plantation house that had been renovated into overnight lodging for tourists. We were in transit from one shaman to another, were very tired, and were looking forward to a peaceful night in a real bed.

During the night, Shirl had a dream about a woman who seemed to be showing her around the house and grounds as though it were still a private residence. Having been provided no specific details beyond our room number when we checked in, Shirl had no prior knowledge of the original owners of the large estate or the people who had previously resided there.

The next morning, intrigued by what had been revealed in the dream, Shirl began to ask questions of the English-speaking staff. Unaware of her dream, the manager provided Shirl with details that corroborated information that the matronly woman in her dream had shared. Directed to a large portrait, Shirl was shocked to see an image of a matriarchal woman—a woman who was identical to her guide on the nighttime tour.

Could this have been merely a coincidence?

One of the most publicly documented dramatic psychic dreams involving the future, however, concerned Rita, another good friend of mine. It's a story that has been printed in books, told numerous times on national television, and that merits quick encapsulation here.

Years ago, Rita was a research scientist doing pioneering work on high-energy rocket propellants in the chemistry laboratory of one of our country's foremost aerospace firms. Ed, a friend and co-worker, began having a reoccurring dream—unusual for a man who seldom remembered his dreams, let alone put any stock in them.

The dream involved him sitting without his lab coat or protective gear in the office area of his laboratory doing paperwork, at which time he would hear an explosion and eventually Rita's screams coming from the adjacent lab. Each time he had the dream, he would rush to the door and call out Rita's name, although he could never see anyone through the dense smoke and fire. He would then step into the burning inferno, unprotected by flame-retardant clothing or face shield, where he would discover Rita lying on the floor, her body engulfed in flames. He would pull her out by one foot, the only portion of her body not burning, and drag her under a deluge shower in the adjacent laboratory. He would then run out from that laboratory into the hall and pick up the red emergency phone . . . .

The dream repeated over and over, each time ending exactly the same way—he saved her life without taking on personal injury of his own. He didn't think to warn Rita—why would he? They were just bad dreams.

One day, while some of Rita's labmates were on a coffee break, Ed was in his lab finishing a report. Suddenly he heard a loud explosion followed by Rita's screams. He rushed to the doorway of her lab to see the *exact* scene he had viewed so often in his recurring dream. Smoke, fumes, and fire obstructed his view. He called out her name and went into her lab. He didn't think of the danger, or of his dreams. He simply acted like an automaton, playing out the dream once again—exactly as he had dreamed it all those nights. He discovered Rita's body in flames, except for one foot, and pulled her out to safety. Although she was badly burned, he was unhurt and his quick reflex had saved her life.

Ed would be the first to tell you that without the dream, he never would have entered the room. No one would have dared to risk it. He said that his dreams were like dress rehearsals preparing him to do something he would otherwise never have done.

Before the accident, Ed had never told anyone about his dreams—not even Rita. But immediately after it occurred, he told a coworker, "I knew it was going to happen."

So—are dreams a meaningless experience?

A psychic dream saved that dear lady's life . . . .

chapter 19

The Psychic Community

PSYCHIC MESSAGES ARE received in many forms. They can involve past-life experiences, present reality, or even future events. They can originate from the spirit world or from another individual on the planet. They can be received by the specific individual to whom they are directed or be picked up by anyone sensitive to psychic energy.

As you know, the more emotionally connected to an issue you are, the more intense the psychic vibrations that you perceive are likely to be.[1] A young mother is, for instance, far more receptive to the desperate needs of her children than a casual friend of the family or stranger. Important communication from your spiritual hierarchy packs greater intensity (and is therefore more easily perceptible) than the intention of a bluffing poker player across the table.

Those living close to nature are generally more tuned in to this metaphysical communication than are we who live in the consumer oriented United States. This is true for a number of reasons. Members of a more primitive society do not contend with the distractions and demands that are prevalent in our lives. Their world does not revolve around the hectic pace of car-pooling children hither and yon or rushing between closely scheduled appointments. They are not as exposed to the energy emissions of neighborhood electrical power lines and radiation from computers, nor do they have to breathe the carbon monoxide resulting from daily travel on crowded freeways. They do not embrace the self-imposed stress of running a large business in order to maintain their cash-gulping social status.

Primitive cultures provide an opportunity for us to learn not only about nurturing a healthy community in lieu of our own egos, they also provide an excellent model for how psychic communication can make a community strong.

The Art of Unconventional Communication

In small rural communities on the African continent, families and villagers come together daily in economic and emotional harmony. This commitment to work in unanimity results in a powerful psychic connection among community members.

While Shirl and I were in Africa, we witnessed the Massai warriors' keen sense of psychic knowing as they walked through the bush armed only with a spear. We savored the harmony of their

---

1. Also, the less objective you may be. See chapter 16 for further discussion.

common thought—the need for spoken words between these people seemed often unnecessary. Also, we observed that they intuitively knew when one of their own was approaching danger.

We observe this same ability to know and feel things without verbal communication in animals and call it *instinct*. Let's call it what it is: a form of intuition or a psychic sense. This knowing comes naturally to those humans who live in the moment and are fully integrated into the environment, people, and objects around them.

Tune Into the Moment—and Listen

Unfortunately, we who reside in the fast-paced developed world generally spend so much time reliving the past or worrying about the future that we often miss the moment. However, anyone who has sky-dived, bungie-jumped, or experienced being in an automobile seconds before an accident can tell you how intense—and how long—a moment can be.

The truth is that the only time that truly exists is the moment: *now*. There is always another tomorrow to replace yesterday's tomorrow. Fretting about yesterday's events will not change the physical outcome of whatever it was that transpired.

The African people living on the land demonstrate that nature has a way of teaching us if we would just *listen*. We Westerners, too, can gain knowledge through our surroundings by just attuning our thoughts to them. Spend several days alone in the outdoors and just listen to the energy of the living objects around you. You will begin to understand. Ask the trees and animals a question and see what answer you receive. Seek the knowledge that the universe can share with you—if only you were to inquire.

The African Shaman: Master of Communication

While Shirl and I were in Tanzania, Africa, we joined an animal-viewing safari led by Jim Heck, a well-known author, guide, and teacher of indigenous lifestyles. As you might have expected, my innate resistance and fear of the unknown had created less than overwhelming enthusiasm for a jaunt off into what I expected to be beyond the remote outskirts of domesticity. Much to my surprise, I encountered the primary roots of our civilization—and an activation of my sense of "beingness."

It was an eye-opening adventure, ultimately paving the way for our Ecuadorian trip, which was to follow. We underwent some unusual experiences—the kind of things that aren't really available in the upper-scale suburbs of California. We ventured within ten feet of a pride of lions during fervent mating season, survived the charge of a large elephant herd and were blown off course and subsequently "lost" on a hot air balloon ride over the Serengeti plains. Other than those incidents and the experience of sleeping in paper-thin tents in areas frequented by wild, man-eating predators, it was a rather commonplace trip.

One reason for our excursion was to meet African shamans and study their ways, just as we had done with other shamans throughout North and South America. We did eventually meet several spiritual healers, but the language barrier prevented us from being able to communicate beyond the superficial. African shamans are generally more guarded around newcomers and less willing to share than other shamans throughout the world. I had been warned that to generate a serious encounter I might have to sit in the wilderness for days, possibly weeks, and wait for them to find me. You probably know by now what chance there would be of me doing *that*.

Jim introduced us to several ancient shamanic sacred sites in the remoteness of the Serengeti plain. Then one morning, we set out to immerse ourselves in the migratory energy of a million and a half wildebeests on the hoof during their annual trek to the Mara, in nearby Kenya. Wildebeests, as you might know, are strange looking animals that appear to have been assembled from spare parts lifted from an early Dr. Suess book. They all mass in one area and then, by instinct, begin to move as one—the precision makes a person wonder whether there is some sort of signaling device built into their unusual bodies. The number of animals was so large that it took us several hours just to drive across the *width* of the herd.

After spending the morning following this assemblage of livestock, we stopped for lunch at an outcropping of rocks. This outcrop had all the signs of being a spiritual site: a large rock mound was the visual center of an enormous open area and nearby trees grew in circular patterns. There was evidence of ancient rock art and the man-made caves at the site gave us the impression of a shamanic ceremonial area. One nearby rock had been carved into the shape of a large-breasted pregnant woman—the worldwide symbol of the Goddess and quite likely a feminine sacred place for birthing or conception.

We left our driver waiting in the vehicle, and Jim led us to a plateau near the top of the mound. The rocky ledge was completely barren, with the exception of a large stone that had been placed near the edge of a sheer drop to the valley below. Jim hunted for a heavy stick which he then handed to Shirl, asking her to beat on the rock as one might play a large drum. The resultant reverberation varied in pitch and tone depending on where and how the surface of the stone was struck.

"There's an interesting story about this rock," Jim said confidentially, lowering his voice as though he wished not to be overheard. The fact that there was no one within fifty miles of us seemed to adequately guarantee the privacy of this conversation.

"It is said that the tribal chiefs would gather here from hundreds of miles around after being summoned by one of the shamans. Even during times of tribal wars, it was considered a sacred and safe place to come together and discuss their differences."

"How would they know to gather?" Shirl asked, joking that fax machines and cellular telephones were not a staple of their society. Knowing that Shirl was a dream worker, Jim smiled as though he had been waiting for her question.

"They knew it from their dreams."

He went on to explain that when a chief desired a high-level meeting, the tribal shaman would come to this rock, enter an altered state of consciousness, and beat on the drum in the dark of night. The shamans of nearby communities would hear the sounds of the drumming *in their dreams* and inform their chief of the conclave.

"It had to have been a really loud noise," I suggested, reasoning that the tribes most likely lived a great distance from one another.

"I don't think so—" Jim replied, calling our attention to the driver, still sitting in the car at the base of the rock.

"When Shirl beats the rock, he doesn't even look up. He can't hear it from *there* with his earth-bound ears."

The abilities of rural shamans seem to be endless.

chapter 20

Gotta Love the Skeptics

ONE DOES NOT necessarily have to be a devout believer in metaphysical phenomenon to experience an extrasensory event. My sudden and unexpected psychic opening in a San Francisco restaurant almost twenty years ago is testimonial to the fact. Prior to that dramatic experience, I was an ardent disbeliever—one who would argue that psychic events were akin to stage illusion: entertaining, but a clear-cut extension of trickery, deception, and wishful thinking.

A skeptic often does not recognize a psychic incident for what it is—but just as belief in the validity of the phenomenon is not a prerequisite for it to occur, it is also not a requirement for one to gain *some* value from it. For example, although we may not consciously perceive a precognitive dream as a forerunner of a future incident, our subconscious will often act on the information and subtly alter our actions to our advantage.

Opening Yourself to Maximum Gain

To gain *maximum* benefit from extrasensory events—or from a psychic reading—the one receiving the information is best served by believing that accessing their higher truth through metaphysical means is possible.

During a psychic reading, the wisdom that comes through the channel will only be as good or valuable to the degree that both parties are open to it. If a client is determined to challenge everything that is being said in order to validate a preconceived notion that psychics are fraudulent con artists, they will no doubt be successful. Not only will they block the flow of energy, but they will not hear or seriously consider what is being presented to them.

Ever have a conversation with someone who is so intent on formulating their response that they don't hear what you're saying? How can you expect to communicate successfully with anyone who has already built impenetrable barriers to the concept that you wish to share? A psychic reading is no different than a conversation. Both sides must be in concert before significant value can be generated.

This tendency for successful readings to happen through collaborative effort is why psychics do not generally perform well when being tested (as though in a sterile laboratory) by those who don't believe in the phenomenon. The scenario is similar to appearing in front of a lynch mob and expecting them to laugh at your jokes.

Now, that's not to say that one has to be completely gullible and automatically accept at face value everything said by someone claiming to be psychic. Naturally, we all need to be discerning about what we are being presented—but not to the point of being closed to the possibility that your truth is accessible by paranormal means.

When in doubt, listen to your inner voice and follow your heart.

The Power of Negative Thinking

Not long ago, I spoke to a ladies group as a promotional effort for my first book. At the conclusion of my presentation, I offered a few mini-readings in order to illustrate the means by which information is attainable during one of my sessions. I was apprehensive about a demonstration on this particular evening, since I felt most of those in attendance were resistant to the concepts that I was presenting.

My concern was not whether what I would channel would be correct or not, but whether I would actually be *heard*. If the subject of the reading is not willing to accept and understand what is being channeled for them, the energy becomes distorted and the information will most likely be met with disbelief. The risk, of course, is that others observing the psychic effort will form skeptical views as a result of a poor presentation, which would be a disservice to everyone in attendance.

I informed the woman who volunteered to be read that one of her strongest spiritual directives was to be more playful and carefree in this incarnation. Her guides indicated that she had been extremely burdened with financial restraints and physical hardships in several of her most recent past lives. This current embodiment was about discovering her inner child as well as personal freedom. Her face displayed a patronizing smile and she emphatically shook her head no, glancing to others in her group for support.

Undaunted, I reiterated that she was to seek personal enjoyment and be more playful. I also mentioned that one of her previous difficult incarnations had taken place in a high altitude and, as a result, she had strong negative feelings relating to mountains and rugged terrain.

She sprang to her feet and triumphantly announced that I was dead wrong. She said she was not "childlike" and was highly insulted at the insinuation that she was not mature. This life was not easy, she patiently explained, and nothing I said pertained to her. She finished by adding that I was wrong about the mountains, too.

"Oh?" I responded.

"Yes," she continued, "I *hate* the mountains!"

"That's the point," I said. "Because of the past life of austerity *in* the mountains, you have a strong emotional connection to them. In this life, you are probably reminded of the difficult life you previously experienced there and as a result, your body reacts negatively to being in mountainous surroundings. That's why we often have unexplainable emotions about things or places we can't otherwise rationalize."

"But I don't even *like* the mountains," she repeated emphatically and sat down.

Hello?

Later I was informed that her husband had an incredibly successful business and they lived in an exclusive neighborhood, suggesting that life was not all that difficult—at least not financially. The icing on the cake was learning that they collected expensive toys such as pinball machines and rare board games and displayed them proudly in their home. Seemed like playfulness and freedom to me . . . .

However, despite the physical and emotional evidence, she was not about to hear what was being presented to her.

It is interesting to note that the objects or experiences we react to strongly, either positively or negatively, are often keys to understanding a past-life experience. When I inform a client that, say, they drowned in a past incarnation, it doesn't surprise me if they respond that they have an extreme fear of water. If I should notify them that they were trapped in a cave in another life, they will most likely admit that they are extremely claustrophobic in this one.

Linking a past life to a known fear often provides the realization that enables us to break old patterns we have outgrown. One of the most successful ways to accomplish this transformation is to just *let go* of the old behavior, the old beliefs. A conscious attempt to logically manipulate or alter outmoded behavior or beliefs that no longer serve us is like patching something best discarded.

The Mission for Singular Truth
(Mission: Impossible)

Unfortunately, we often attempt to use the strong-arm "change-the-other-guy" method when the beliefs of others appear to be in conflict with our own. We tend to feel threatened when someone else does not subscribe to *our* truth. We often attempt to convince others that they're wrong in order that *we* might feel safer.

I recall meeting up with a number of young religious missionaries in Ecuador as we were en route to the Andes, fresh from living with the peaceful residents of the rain forest. These travelers were all clean-cut American kids in their late teens and early twenties. They were full of enthusiasm for their mission, and were actively distributing information on their church doctrine. The group was expounding their spiritual view to all who would listen—dedicated to eradicating the false doctrines subscribed to by these isolated, "ignorant" cultures. False doctrines were, of course, defined as anything that differed from *their* religious liturgy, salted with *their* righteous interpretation.

They called themselves medical missionaries but, when questioned, admitted that they had no more than superficial first-aid training. Their sole purpose was to convert what they called the "unenlightened, indigenous natives" to what the mission claimed to be the truth. They spoke of the poor, unhappy people whom they had "saved" with their religious logic and economic bribery. To hear the missionaries tell it, all who reside in the rain forest of the Third World live in extreme poverty and squalor and lack moral values. The "illiterate population" were an unhappy lot before their conversion, the missionaries boasted, but had now been squared away thanks to the efforts of their unselfish crusade.

I was under the impression that the native population consists of a happy and carefree people who perceive themselves as an integral part of a self-reliant community. They live in harmony with their peaceful, ethereal temperament as they honor the ecological balance of nature. Their way of being works just fine for them and the roots of their ecological and spiritual values allows them to live a meaningful life in their own unique and special way. Were we observing the same people? Is our culture so pompous as to insist that our collective belief system and manner of life are superior to any other?

Now, I know that these young, purpose-serving missionaries had traveled to Ecuador with only good intentions. They believed they were there to *assist* the less educated and less advanced by introducing their belief system—but who are we to determine that *our* way of being is best for someone else? Sure, *I* would rather live in a world of modern medicine, instant communication and wide screen TV with surround sound. That works for *me* . . . but it might not if I lived off of the land in the center of an entirely different environment. Our economy and lifestyle is different from others. Our culture is based on an entirely different set of principles and values than other cultures.

Furthermore, guess what happens when the Western-educated white man loses interest and leaves? His religion often fails to meet the spiritual needs of those he converted.

The missionaries are a good example of a group of intellectuals who are ignorant about the unique nature of the native's spiritual views and what provides them with their extraordinary and invaluable life force. Missionaries who insist that the natives' belief system is invalid are the same as the non-believer who pontificates the diatribe that psychic experiences are nothing more than superstitious folklore.

Be open to concepts you don't understand. Just because you're ignorant of something doesn't mean it isn't true or real. People who insisted that the world was flat even after Columbus and Galileo proved otherwise were unwilling to accept a new point of view. Can the same be said of those who believe that reality is only as they *see* it?

If you never were brave enough to try ice cream, *imagine* what you might have missed!

I remember a phrase an Eastern seer once told me years ago when I asked for a response to pass on to those with a negative outlook:

> *If you come to me with doubts, I will give you every*
> *reason to be doubtful. If you come to me with love, I*
> *will show you more than you have ever known.*

chapter 21

Descent to the Lower World

ALTHOUGH I ENCOURAGE you to open yourself to new psychic experiences, consciously setting out to explore the occult world of ghosts and negative forces face to face is not something I heartily recommend. True, I have crossed paths with my share of spirit forms since I became a professional psychic, but generally it has been either because someone requested my assistance or an apparition initiated the connection. In the case of the young boy's essence haunting the doctor's house, or the violent energy roaming the corridors of the Gold Country bed and breakfast, I only intervened to reestablish spiritual harmony for both the living and the spirit visitor.

I have always felt that purposely invoking the energy of a random ghost just for the fun of it is dangerous. The problem is, you have *no* control over who might show up.

Still, after Shirl's positive experience in the manteum, I decided that I had to try it out for myself. I guess curiosity got the best of me—along with the thought that I had had no spirit contact with my father in the two years since his death. Not having sensed his presence really surprised me, since I worked closely with him in the family business and was very much like him—a product of his thinking and personality as well as his DNA.

Following much soul searching, I phoned Dee and made an appointment to visit her manteum for the express purpose of contacting my dad . . . should he be interested.

The **Manteum**

It was a dark and stormy night . . . (I always wanted to write that phrase in a book)—rather an appropriate kind of evening for my spooky entrance into the foreboding ways of the spirit world. The winter rains had been plentiful and I had to forge streams and climb mountains in order to reach Dee's home. Well . . . maybe not forge streams—there was some minor flooding on the freeway. And I guess her steep driveway didn't *quite* constitute a mountain—but when you begin a paragraph with *It was a dark and stormy night*, I think one is allowed to embellish a bit.

In any case, I was warmly welcomed into Dee's house by her husband and immediately seated in a comfortable downstairs family room. She entered the room moments later and, after polite conversation, asked me to fill out a brief questionnaire.

First we reviewed some preliminary guidelines and I listened to an account regarding several ghosts Dee had recently encountered in the very room where we were seated. Then I followed Dee upstairs to the area containing the black curtained cubicle. She sat me down on a chair that had been placed inside the enclosure and went over the last-minute instructions. She advised me to relax and make like a reporter, observing what took place rather than expecting to be in the center of the action. She assured me that I would be okay and that she would come back and check on me in forty-five minutes or so.

Dee closed the curtain and as she departed the room, she mumbled something—probably some ancient ceremonial good luck mantra or a verse of Gregorian chant—though it was hard to tell, since a large clap of thunder and a temporary dimming of the lights dramatically accented her exit.

I sat there and looked around the darkened space. As my eyes slowly adjusted to the low light in the chamber, I began to make out the same mirror and frame Shirl had described from her ayahuasca experience in the rain forest. An eerie dim light had been projected onto the draperies covering the rear wall and the reflection viewed in the looking glass set a frightening and sinister tone.

My heart was beating faster as I began to recognize the timely arrival of my old, familiar companion—Mr. Fear—who had accompanied me on many previous uncharted adventures. Although I had come to this place in order to expand my metaphysical experience, I began to question the intellectual reasoning that had placed me in the midst of this frightening moment. It seemed that encountering a ghost unexpectedly was quite different than setting up an appointment to see one and then dealing with the anticipation.

There was a part of me that desired contact with my dad and his mother, my grandmother—the white-haired German lady who psychics have repeatedly observed in my energy field. She died over forty years ago, but I have been informed on numerous occasions that it was her spirit who successfully guided me past the potential emotional pitfalls following my sudden psychic opening. On top of that, she was the only grandparent I ever knew. I have fond childhood memories of our brief time together.

However, a larger part of my psyche was quite apprehensive about the possible sudden appearance of unsolicited and frightening apparitions that might spring from the depths of the blackness at any moment. I can easily recall childhood memories of evil, ghoul-like images. I knew that these forces lay unseen, waiting to emerge from the dark corners of my room while I anxiously wished for sleep to take me somewhere safe. Believing that the boogie man was hiding under my bed was fearful enough without having to deal with the lurking shadows I strongly suspected lived on the edge of the unknown.

Perched on a chair in a darkened room anticipating contact by a wayward resident of the spirit world provides plenty of fodder to activate the imagination of the ever-present child trapped in the body of this fifty-something adult. I soon found that my state of mind was being actively consumed by Mr. Fear rather than focusing on my original objective: conversing with the spirit of my father. The recurring claps of thunder and the sound of rain pounding on the roof made the evening even more foreboding. I began to pull the imaginary bed covers over my head as I had done as a small child. Meanwhile, I counted the widely spaced minutes until Dee finally returned to extricate me from my scary predicament. It seemed like hours.

She seemed surprised that I had not seen or sensed anything of a paranormal nature. I had to admit that I was puzzled as well, having experienced more than a half dozen unsolicited apparitions since metaphysically awakening in my late thirties.

As I left her house I drew in a long, deep breath from the rain-cleaned night air. I had mixed emotions. I was somewhat disappointed that I had not met my father, but greatly relieved that nothing frightening had taken place. Dee assured me that I could return at a later date at no additional cost, since my expectations had not been fulfilled. I thanked her and told her I would call her, knowing deep down that I intended to leave well-enough alone.

A Second Chance

Several months later, I met Dee at a gathering of the same metaphysical group that had provided the opportunity for our original encounter.

"You know you can revisit my manteum anytime you're ready," she reminded me softly.

I don't think so, came my mental reply. I say mental because Amy found her way to the inner-body mechanism that interprets my thoughts into spoken words and rewired it so that I heard my voice say with firm assurance,

"Sure—why not?"

Before I knew it, I had booked another session.

We agreed on a daytime appointment. It felt more user friendly than encountering the uncharted corners of the manteum at night. I knew the box would be just as dark, but some kind of twisted logic suggested that the scary apparitions may be asleep during the daytime, so it would be far less terrifying if I knew the sun was shining outside.

I arrived at her house at the appointed hour, just as an unpredicted downpour began to deposit raindrops on my windshield.

Uh oh, I thought, wondering if a dark and stormy *day* had the same kind of impact.

Dee met me at the door and welcomed me. She seemed anxious to share several additional ghostly encounters that had taken place in her house since my previous visit. One involved the spirit of her deceased father, who likes to repeatedly hide her mother's gardening gloves. Dee claimed that each time the gloves are finally found, her deceased father has playfully reconstructed one of them so that they both are configured to fit the same hand.

Delightful, I thought, *All I need are ghosts who want to mess around with my energy.*

Then she shifted her attention to the purpose of my visit.

"Tell me about your father and grandmother," she said, referring to some notes she had taken during our previous session. "Describe their physical appearance along with a sound or smell you associate with either one."

"Smell?" I asked.

"Often sounds and fragrances come through first," she responded. "It's not just about sight."

Of course, I knew she was right. I quickly inventoried the numerous encounters I have had with ghosts and recalled that most of my experiences activated more than just the visual sense. The ghosts I discovered years ago in a London pub had created a musty smell. The spirit of the young boy I encountered in a castle in Germany had made a whooshing sound as he rapidly moved around the room. Shirl's father, who visited us shortly after he died in 1982, brought a pungent smell of cigar smoke and diesel oil—two odors Shirl had said were a daily part of his life.

I thought about the images of the two souls I wished to contact and wondered whether they still had a connection with the earth plane and were willing to drop by for a visit. I remembered the smell of bread baking in my grandmother's oven on my frequent visits to her country house as a child. I thought of the sounds my father made as I synchronized my breathing with his while his spirit prepared to vacate his energy-depleted and worn-out physical body just prior to his passing.

Dee's voice suddenly brought me back to the present moment as she mumbled something about only allowing friendly spirits into her house. She promised that nothing fearful would occur, and suggested that I let go of any apprehension I had and simply provide the space for whatever was to happen.

"Fear," she reminded me in a stern tone, "only serves to block spiritual energy."

Let go of the fear?

Mr. Fear and I had traveled the road of life together. We were inseparable—like Abbott and Costello . . . salt and pepper . . . politicians and corruption . . . .

With a nod of her head, she indicated that it was time to do what I had come to do. I once again followed her up the stairs and into the room containing the manteum. It looked a bit more friendly in daylight but, by the time the window curtains in the room were drawn and the black-draped container was sealed, it was plenty dark.

"I choose not to let Mr. Fear affect my experience," I said to myself bravely, once she left the room. As I had done with the Fate Guy, I needed to disassociate my energy from his influence.

I observed the mirror in front of me. Dee had informed me that I needn't constantly and intently stare into it. I began to breath more deeply, altering my gaze to "soft eyes," as one does when attempting to view an aura.

All of my previous experiences with ghosts have been primarily to *sense* their presence rather than literally view them. With that in mind, I decided to let go of conceptualizing the mirror as a physical reflection of what can be seen.

Imagine it as a window or doorway to a new experience, I heard Joel (my pensive guide with the mismatched socks) suggest in his matter-of-fact way.

It was then that I began my descent.

The room had somehow suddenly transformed into an elevator and the mirror had the semblance of a window to another world. As I sat frozen in my chair, I felt as though I was sinking into a lower room and the mirror-window was rising above me. I blinked my eyes in order to assure myself that I could return the window to its accustomed position and, for a brief moment, reconnect to what I knew physical reality to be.

After forcing the mirror to go back to its proper place, I allowed the descending sensation to return. I knew the inner journey experience had begun. Joel reminded me that what I was about to experience was *my* reality—*my* illusion.

Almost immediately, I began to sense four or five foreign presences in the room and could plainly observe bits of the swirling green mist that spiritualists and mediums refer to as *ectoplasm*. The wisps broke apart and joined with other pockets of similar vapor as though floating in slow motion in some sort of thick atmosphere.

Two hooded dancing figures appeared in the foreground, gently swaying to some distant, indiscernible music. I could view them against the dimly lit black backdrop—they appeared to have been projected onto the surface of the green mist, like a hologram. The haze came together and separated, seemingly choreographed by an unseen consciousness.

Then I saw the eyes of what some refer to as the Gatekeeper. He was a wee-sized creature with white piercing eyes, and he looked to be a cross between one of the Seven Dwarfs and R2-D2 from the *Star Wars* trilogy.

The Gatekeeper seemed passive and non-threatening, and his unblinking eyes seemed to observe my every thought as though it were in a cartoon bubble above my head. He gave me the impression that he was monitoring the movement of ethereal energy through some sort of passageway leading to another dimension.

My focus changed and I became aware of a small white cottage attached to a medieval tower, like two fairy tale structures had somehow become fused together. I knew on some level that my dad was inside the gingerbread cottage, having worked his way out of the confines of the tower. It seemed that he wanted to be by himself, apparently to reflect on where his passage from physical life had deposited him. I felt that he, too, was confronting his fear. I was coming to understand that we both had been placed on this earth to initiate a means of escape from our personal limitations.

I also was certain that he was not yet ready to communicate with me directly. I knew on some level that he was okay, busily discovering the depth of the emotional and spiritual inner peace that had partially eluded him in his last incarnation. I could begin to better appreciate the worldwide shamanic teachings that characterize our physical incarnation as a workshop—a path designed to provide an opportunity to grow and advance spiritually. All the more reason we must discover our life's purpose, experience the depth of our personal potential, and complete the karma carried forward to this lifetime while we still have time.

I heard a noise outside the room that housed the manteum and the "elevator" began to rise. Midway through the experience I had become aware that in addition to the Gatekeeper, there was a doorman—a guardian—just outside the entrance to the manteum. This new sound seemed to be the doorman's method of announcing that this Disneyland-style E-ticket ride was coming to an end.

As I completed my ascent to present-world reality, I realized that I had been in the lower world—the realm shamans describe as a place of power animals and subconscious reality. The lower world is not to be confused with Hell, nor the upper world with Heaven—labels that some interpreters of Christianity associate with morality levels assigned on Judgment Day.

Then Dee knocked on the door to the outer room and my connection was severed. As she assisted me from the enclosure, I asked about the dwarf and doorman.

"The Gatekeeper? You saw the Gatekeeper?"

"Yes, I guess I did!" I wasn't surprised that she seemed to know to whom I had referred. I recalled that Shirl had viewed the mirror as a doorway and it seemed logical that doorways might also require gatekeepers.

"The man outside the manteum was probably *my* dad," she tossed out matter-of-factly. "I asked him to watch over you."

When we returned downstairs for debriefing, I shared my experience in greater detail. I informed her that the manteum was much more friendly this time and that it had provided me an opportunity to face my fear—and let it go.

Her smile was filled with understanding.

"I didn't *see* my dad per se, but I knew he was there in the white cottage," I continued. "I felt my grandmother's presence and her daughter—my aunt—as well."

"Honor what you have learned . . . what you have experienced," Dee said.

She proceeded to throw in a few other pat phrases and words of encouragement. I think I only half heard her, since I was watching my guides gleefully exchanging high fives, pleased that I had taken on Mr. Fear—and won!

chapter 22

The Anatomy of Fear

IT'S TIME THAT we look at this fear thing in more detail. Fear is the one emotion that most often suppresses our inherent extrasensory abilities. It can be a major obstacle to discovering our true identity and exploring our perception of reality.

Fear is often a major player in life-defining moments. It can keep us alive by alerting us to danger. However, it also has the potential to become extremely harmful when it dominates and controls our every thought and action.

Fear is most often construed as a negative and limiting emotion. We've all experienced it: fear of the dark, fear of failure, fear of taking a risk. It often hampers us from being truly *present,* attaching us to past actions, replaying old behavior tapes, and causing us to react in familiar but limiting patterns.

Fear was the most significant passion that I had to battle during my initial psychic opening. It has consistently tested me along my path toward spiritual and psychic growth. Examples include my resistance in the Ecuadorian rain forest and my near panic in the darkened manteum. Fear prevented the reluctant woman at the lecture from hearing the helpful karmic-reducing directive issued from her guides. It obstructed the young boy's spirit in the doctor's house from finding his way to the white light. It's what would have hindered Rita's lab associate from saving her life if it were not for his repetitive precognitive dreams.

Fear can easily become a way of life, given half a chance.

Of course, fear can be a positive experience too—a forerunner of personal growth. During the ayahuasca ceremony, it was an indispensable part of my spiritual initiation into a higher level of understanding. It has instigated many an adrenaline rush, alerting me to potential danger. It has been an educational tool, delineating personal weaknesses and challenging me to instigate positive changes in my personal behavior.

However you experience it, fear is destined to be an attention-getter in one form or another. It was a certainly a close companion on my first day of kindergarten. It was ever present during the opening moments of my television shows. It was in my throat when I proposed marriage—both times!

And it certainly accompanied my initial psychic experience nearly twenty years ago . . . .

The **Moment** of **Truth**

At one time, I was a charter member among genuine skeptics—a building contractor for heaven's sake. I was a logical, left-brain reasoning human being who depended strictly on his five senses to define a world view. Emotionally unprepared for an event not deemed even remotely possible, my unexpected psychic experience was a terrifying moment.

I was enjoying dinner in a posh San Francisco restaurant with new friends. We had become acquainted during a three-day workshop designed to enhance self-image and creative potential. The seminar had been quite an eye-opening experience and, as a result, I had been jolted awake to my own sensitivity in a way I never knew was possible before. All of a sudden, while finishing my meal, I *knew* that a woman across the room—a woman I had never seen before— was about to leap to her feet and desperately gasp for air. She would then stop breathing and fall to the floor, unconscious.

When it happened moments later, it scared the you-know-what out of me.

Confusion and stark terror coursed through my body immediately following this bizarre and scary incident. How did I know what was about to happen before it occurred? Had I somehow caused it by merely thinking about it? Was this the work of some sort of witchcraft, black magic, or perhaps the devil himself?

If I had allowed the overwhelming fear to control and dominate my actions in the weeks that followed, I would not have pursued the nagging inner desire to learn more—the need to understand what had happened . . . and whether it would occur again. I would have lost the opportunity to seek and acquire the knowledge that eventually led to the development of my psychic ability and the acquisition of new metaphysical tools. This abrupt turn in my life directly contributed to the advancement of my spiritual understanding and the eventual resolution of past-life karma. All of this because I didn't allow Mr. Fear to dictate my reactions.

Beyond Fear: The Road to Insight

Confronting events that we cannot comprehend is generally difficult and frightening. Encountering a ghost, confronting the concept of dying, or jettisoning your old and familiar limitations can be scary occurrences. On a grander scale, James Redfield, author of *The Celestine Prophecy* (Warner Books, 1993) and *The Tenth Insight* (Warner Books, 1996), suggests that the fear that our culture faces as it moves from a focus on material reality to a transformed spiritual world view needs to be addressed and dissipated before the truth of our experience can be fully understood. Society as a whole typically clings to what is familiar, resists change, and seeks to control, eliminate, or avoid what it does not comprehend.

On the other hand, many indigenous societies have used fear to *advance* a neophyte's spiritual maturity and develop his or her character. They have created and perpetuated ceremonies to test the courage of their young men and women during the transition from puberty to adulthood by requiring the initiate to confront a personal fear. Having to navigate through an underwater obstacle course, as was required of Egyptian initiates, is a well-documented example. Jumping headfirst from a tall tree with an untested vine wrapped around one's ankles, confronting a wild animal, or facing a tribal enemy to prove one's worthiness was common to many ancient cultures. In light of the absolute lack (and disdain) for such practices in our culture today, I think venturing off into the wilderness on a vision quest to directly confront my fears and find my true self (as I did at age fifty-something) exceeded the modern-day criteria.[1]

A Vision Quest

My story begins like many you've read. Once upon a time . . . a few years ago . . . in a kingdom far, far away . . . there lived this bright,

---

1. Okay—so I wasn't exactly entering puberty when I got around to doing this, but hey—better late than never, I always say.

handsome young prince (it's my story so I may have taken a *small* liberty or two in this brief preamble).

Actually, a friend of mine approached me one evening with an intriguing idea. He asked if I wanted to be included in a vision quest he was organizing. It was to take place in the far reaches of the Sierra mountains in California. He intended to invite a few mutual male friends and wanted to know if I would be interested in being included in this experience. It was something I had read about and considered doing from time to time. However, not being a wilderness camping enthusiast, it had been moved well down on my priority list of things I had to accomplish in this lifetime (I think it was somewhere between wrestling alligators and bungie jumping, but I'm not sure).

After much contemplation, I concluded that if I was ever going to do it, this would be the time, place, and companions that would make me most comfortable. The deciding factor was: if my friends were willing to do it, I certainly didn't want to miss out.

There are many books explaining the goals of a vision quest and how to go about undertaking one. Its principal purpose, of course, is to isolate oneself from the busy work-a-day world in order to discover one's true inner self, or soul essence, on a level not generally accessible in our hectic and high-pressure lifestyle. Typically, a young initiate in a Native American community ventures alone into the depths of nature for a prolonged period of time and fasts, seeking a vision to provide insight into their true nature. They are said to leave as children and return as adults—often with a new name and an increased sense of purpose.

The true believers probably set off with nothing but the clothes on their backs, but our group amended it a bit by each taking a sleeping bag, a change of clothing, a filtered water pump, a drum or musical instrument, and personal medical essentials (like a snakebite kit). No food, books, battery-operated televisions, laptop computers, or diversionary items were allowed. My cell phone was decidedly ruled out.

We found four others of like mind who wished to go, and then set a date. We also invited a mutual acquaintance who had been on vision quests in the past to hold base camp and be available in the event of an emergency.

It was decided that the event would begin with a sweat lodge ceremony—an ancient Native American ritual of purification still practiced in many parts of the world. The purpose of this event was to set our intentions and offer prayers for the physical and emotional safety of all who were preparing to undertake the potentially fearful and arduous spiritual journey.

After setting up base camp, we constructed a hogan[2] by tying poles together and covering them with blankets that we had carried on our long trek up the mountain. We gathered large stones and placed them into a blazing fire for over six hours, where they were heated to a glowing red-hot temperature before being brought into the lodge.

As night fell, we stood in a circle, each stating what we hoped to gain from the vision quest. My intent was to confront my fears and limitations so that I might grow personally and increase my ability to serve others both spiritually and metaphysically. The sweat lodge ceremony was divided into four sections, each lasting one hour:

1. We honored the process and thanked the universe for the experience.

2. We each stated and discarded the fears we carried to the quest.

3. We said prayers of healing for ourselves and for others important to us.

4. We opened ourselves fully to what we were about to experience.

Between each segment, we brought in additional heated rocks and poured water on them to create billowing hot steam. Native American tradition says that the prayers and affirmations in a sweat lodge ceremony are fulfilled once this vapor is released into the universe. We sealed our intentions by chanting and improvising songs with drums and rattles.

---

2. A traditional earth-covered Navajo structure.

When the ceremony was complete, we were each issued a length of rawhide. Standing naked in a circle in the soft radiance of reflected moonlight, we ceremoniously tied a knot in each of the other's rawhide strand. Each of these strands was to become a necklace. With each twist of the leather we recited an affirmation, adding our individual strength and personal good wishes to the strand of a fellow participant and good friend. As a result, we would each carry the energy of all those whose individual journeys were to separate us for four days.

The next morning, we departed camp in a bond of silence. Three of us had previously decided to head north and the other three south. After hiking to a higher altitude for about an hour, our trio created a circle of rocks to act as a message center. We agreed to visit the designated hoop at separate times each day and add a rock to our individual pile, indicating that we were safe and not in need of assistance. This ritual created not only a bond between us, but provided some peace of mind that we were not totally alone.

Then we split up and went our separate ways.

I found a perfect campsite and set up my tent (you didn't think I was going to sleep out in the open, did you?) on a bluff overlooking a creek, which was to be the source of my water supply. I erected my shelter under several trees in front of an open area about thirty feet square, where I planned to create a medicine wheel. I then spread out a coil of rope in a circle around my campsite. This, I had been told, would discourage my *primary* source of fear (the you-know-whats) from slithering into my space. It would do nothing to discourage hungry bears, but, hey—we each have our priorities.

I had read enough about Native American medicine wheels to decide to use one as the basis to process my vision quest during this sacred experience. I knew that many indigenous nations of the Americas believe that in "sacred time" events don't follow the human rules of linearity. Since past, present, and future all become part of the larger *now*, I anticipated that I would perceive a new kind of reality. Time would no longer be an accurate means of measurement since none of us carried a wristwatch. Meals marking specific portions of a day were eliminated and the normal distractions of life were removed. The medicine wheel would provide the structure I needed to offset the anticipated reality distortion.

When it came to defining directions on the wheel, I decided to create a composite interpretation of various Native American tribal points of view. I designated the East as imaginative, the West as psychological, the North as mental, the South as physical, the earth as mortal, and the sky as spiritual. All directions (as Native American shamans will tell you) become part of the One in the sacred medicine wheel of *now*. In addition, each direction has individually been associated with animals, the time of day, seasons of the year, and so on. For example, some common symbols analogous with the West would include a bear or beaver, evening time, harvest season, the time of parenting and wisdom, the experience of death or letting go, the place of dreams, the enemy of powerlessness and the color black.

Ritualizing the process, I said a prayer and set an intention in each direction on the wheel. I faced East, the direction of the rising sun and newness, and prayed for the dawning light of love and an increased understanding of the sacred ways. I turned to the West—to the rays of the setting sun—and pledged to let loose the old ways that no longer served me. I turned to the North and asked for mystic and ancient mental visions to assist me in my spiritual growth. I turned to the south and prayed for physical safety and the gentleness of a new way of being. Of the earth I asked to be in touch with my mortality so that I might be more aware of my physical journey. In the sky I looked to the Creator Spirit, acknowledging Creator presence in all that surrounded me.

My purpose in performing this opening ritual was to set my intentions, to open myself to a higher plane of consciousness, and to accept the totality of my being. My remaining journey was divided among the energies of the six directions—the four cardinal directions plus the earth below and sky above. All of it occupied the time of *now*.

The total experience turned out to be awesome.

Solitude: A Different Perspective

As you can imagine, I confronted and processed many fears during this spiritual journey. The fear of being alone in the wilderness (I was an hour's distance from the nearest neighboring campsite) was probably at the top of my list. Boredom during the day was a minor concern compared to the feeling of fear and isolation when the sun went down and the shadow of night began to invade my space. During the *loooooooooong* dark nights, I was certain that creatures large and small, displeased that I had invaded their space, were roaming freely outside my tent and arguing about where I fit into the food chain. My greatest worry of all was the invasion fleet of UFOs that I was certain had positioned itself just out of sight, ready to abduct me when the moon disappeared behind a cloud.

By the completion of the first sun cycle, I began to move into a different awareness, discovering a new mindfulness previously unknown to me. It was subtle enlightenment at first, such as the realization that the only small patch of wild flowers to be seen was to the south of my tent—the same direction that the plant kingdom occupies on the medicine wheel. I encountered the playfulness of my inner child, who reminded me that he was alive and well and did not want to be neglected. I spoke to a passing caterpillar, who advised me to proceed slowly, followed by a butterfly who indicated that the process of my transformation was at hand. I befriended the guardian trees that surrounded my campsite in the form of a power circle. I conversed with their auras—a method described in one of the nine insights of *The Celestine Prophecy*.

I came to learn more about the moon—the evening sky's feminine (yin) reflective light source. I found that I thoroughly enjoyed leisurely soaking up the subtle and healing qualities of this outdoor night light—a security often forgotten in the urban world. Since the moon was in its waxing phase, it was truly a time that was conducive to reflecting . . . and manifesting what I needed in my life.

During the four-day quest, I met a new spirit guide—not one of the personal guides with whom I was already familiar, but one who referred to himself as a *universal* guardian spirit. I had prophetic dreams while fully alert during the day, as well as during the sleep cycle at night. I even learned that boiling water over the campfire and pretending that it's a nutritious broth helps to dissipate the hunger pangs.

But most importantly, I discovered that *I could do it*. I could survive the long ordeal without encountering a single snake, a wandering ghost, or a frightening alien creature.

I had faced down the Fear Monster and won. I had advanced into my spiritual adulthood.

On the fifth day, we all returned to the main campsite where we each devoured a huge breakfast and engaged in enthusiastic and endless insightful conversation. Each of us had a different set of stories to share. Each had been moved by unique individual emotions encountered in the isolation of our personal spaces. Each had confronted and processed one or more of our fears.

And each was dramatically changed by the experience.

chapter 23

How to Change the World

BREAKING THROUGH THE confining limitations
perpetuated by lifelong fears can provide numerous
opportunities for personal growth. Discovering that it
is possible to access our intuitive abilities is the first step
toward tuning into the greater cosmic energy. When we
learn more about how to use our natural psychic abilities,
we can more easily perceive the wonders of the universe
and our specific role in the overall scheme of things. As
we access this higher understanding, we gain valuable
insight into who we are—as well as where we are
ultimately headed. In order to best accomplish
this, we first need to determine the purpose
of our current incarnation. When

we know why we have selected our current physical form, gender, and the individual qualities that we see reflected back to us when we look in the mirror, we can resolve our karma more easily. We can move to the next level of spiritual understanding.

If you are not yet aware of your purpose this time around, you can at least be certain about these things:

1. We are not here at the whim, or for the amusement, of the gods.

2. We have quite a bit to say about what happens in our lives.

The **Illusion** of **Everyday Life**

What you may have forgotten when you initially chose this specific incarnation is that life, like a stage play, is just an *illusion*. Imagine for a moment that you are the author, actor, and director in a stage drama. Once you've scripted the play, you can fully immerse yourself in the role you've chosen—*or you can rewrite the part*. All roles are of equal importance, by the way, regardless of the order of billing on the marquee.

Ask yourself: what exactly is reality? Ever notice that your observation of life and the nature of reality is often quite different than someone else's? For example, someone whom you find extremely fascinating may be considered boring by others. What you find tactful or clever might be thought of as bad taste by a good friend. A remembered event may be interpreted quite differently by someone you shared it with.

Reality is defined by the one perceiving it.

Life is an illusion. Pretend stuff. *Mister Roger's Neighborhood*. If you don't like the neighborhood, your options are to live with it, change it, or move out. What you may not have realized until now is that *you* are the principal director of your little melodrama and *you* possess the inherent ability to edit the action and the story line— whenever you choose to learn how.

The Proof Is in the Afterlife

Let's consider reports given by the many people who have been declared clinically dead and then returned to life. Those who have written or spoken of their near-death experiences provide us with a glimpse of how they view Heaven or the after-life. These people consistently describe their experiences in terms that correspond to their religious *expectations*. Those who are faithful to a particular spiritual belief system will generally report meeting a central icon of their religion: Christ, Abraham, Buddha, Vishnu Krishna, etc. Those who are less spiritual will more often encounter a respected historical character or close relative during a near-death experience.

Upon reviewing thousands of documented experiences over the years, we might easily surmise that Heaven—or the spiritual world—conforms to the individual viewpoint of each observer. We can conclude, then, that either 1) there are as many separate heavens as there are souls on this planet, or 2) that we each create a specific *illusion* tailored to our particular belief system.

Let's assume that the same architect that designed Heaven designed the physical realm—and used a similar blueprint for both. If the heavenly experience conforms to what we anticipate it to be, can't we accept the fact that our expectations on the physical plane do the same thing? This physical incarnation is a reflection of our belief system—it is, for all intents and purposes, an illusion. This being so, let's modify our reality by simply changing our beliefs and expectations . . . . let's perceive reality *differently*. Then, like Frank Sinatra, we will all be able to sing . . . *I did it my way!*

Be creative—this year's nominations for Best Manifestation by an Actor in a Leading Role have not yet been finalized . . . .

The **Art** of **Scripting** **Your Own Reality**

Question: Why do the same old tiresome behavior patterns reappear time after time in your life?

Answer: They reoccur because you have accepted them, expected them, and assumed you had no choice. You have instructed the Fate Guy to cast you in the same part, and he will probably continue to provide the old familiar script until you decide to change roles—or change the outcome.

Let's look at this important concept from a different perspective. Certainly, we can all agree that we create and individualize our own dream images. We can also agree that our personal belief system and emotional perspective is a major influence on the tone and theme of our nighttime journeys. It makes sense, then, to assume that once you modify your personal viewpoints, your dreams will begin to reflect those changes as they take hold in the depths of your deeper being. If this makes sense to you, let's carry this thought a step further beginning with two facts that we all readily accept:

1. Dream time is a form of consciousness: a reality.

2. Waking life is a form of consciousness: a reality.

Now—if you can successfully change your dream consciousness . . . is there a pattern here?

Another thing: Have you ever noticed that when you close your eyes at night, everyone else disappears? You're left with *you*. Your entire life adventure has been arranged for your exclusive, personal experience. No one else creates your reality. *You* hold the power— you have total responsibility for the way you perceive reality.

Question: What, then, determines what *is*?

Answer: It is either past-life karma dictating what you need
to be presented in this life or simply your present-
day perception (an illusion) based on how you
have *decided* things must be as a result of your
prior experiences.

So ... if we were to *change* our perceptions—you get the idea.

Determining Your Path

My life is certainly not any more significant than anyone else's. We
are each an equal piece of the whole as far as the universe is concerned. I have never caught a touchdown pass in a big game, faced
death in the defense of my country, or been voted the most likely to
do anything. I'm just an ordinary guy trying to figure out the rules of
the game as I go along, and attempting to minimize my personal
fouls during the process.

Part of my personal karma is to move from my limited, fearful
status to one of greater personal freedom. As a child I was always
(generally) a good boy, eating all (most) of my vegetables and never
(seldom) failing to make parental curfew on time. I was never
(rarely) in trouble, since I was extremely fearful of circumventing the
expectations and authority of others.

Boy, did I need to break free of *those* patterns.

Question: How do we break free? How do we alter our
perceptions and erase our old tapes?

Answer: Face the issue. Decide to change it. Move out of the
neighborhood. Begin by releasing your fears,
limitations, and disbelief. Trust your intuition and
communicate with your inner guidance. Commit
to the development of your psychic abilities and be
clear about discovering what you came here in this
lifetime to resolve. Set goals, be clear about what

you want to accomplish, and begin to manifest it by altering your outdated belief system. Know that *everything* is possible—all you have to do is to ask for it.

Remember: our lifelong patterns repeat themselves in order to provide us with continuing *opportunities* to both confront and change the rules of our game.

Knowing that You Can

Faith plays a major role in this process. Look at what our religious beliefs require of us. Many in the Western world, for example, accept Jesus Christ as their Savior . . . a Messiah—or, at the very least, a prophet, in spite of the fact that there is little or no physical or direct historical evidence that He even existed. There are no photographs that document His physical incarnation. We have no newsreels with which to validate what our major religions expect us to blindly accept. Only our *faith*—our viewpoint—leads us to our personal truth.

Do we see the glass as half-full or half-empty? Depends on our perspective, right?

Reality can be almost anything we want it to be. I am reminded of the time Shirl and I were standing on a burial mound at the top of a high mountain in South America. It was well after dark and we had been led to a little-known destination, where legend says the high priests conducted their sacred work in ancient days. Although this location was now a hilltop that appeared physically indistinguishable from other hilltops, we could still sense the intense nature of the timeless spiritual energy there.

As we approached the site, the sky suddenly darkened. Lightning began to flash as though strobe lights had been activated to dramatically backlight the swirling mist hanging in the night air. The unusual atmospheric conditions provided an eerie glow to the sky and we almost expected to see a UFO descending, like in the final scene of *Close Encounters of the Third Kind.*

Once we arrived at the top, the group we were traveling with became caught up in collecting fragments of numerous ancient arrowheads. These remained from the multitude of bloody battles fought defending this sacred land. Many rival armies had attempted to conquer and control the area for the mystical power it was believed to embody.

Then, dramatically, the mysterious light and sound show suddenly ceased and the night became dark and still. We all gathered together. It seemed that some unseen power had motivated each of us to seek the safety and reassurance of the collective group.

The lantern we carried to illuminate the narrow, muddy trail leading to this powerful place was inexplicably extinguished by an undetected rush of air. We were each drawn to search the sky, expecting a sign—a mystical message from the gods or, perhaps, the early stages of an alien abduction by a hovering spacecraft hidden in the moonless night.

The silent tension was abruptly pierced by the sound of a ringing telephone.

Our indigenous native leader reached under his shawl to retrieve a cell phone from his pocket. He listened for a moment and handed it to Shirl.

"It's for you," he said in broken English.

It was the completion of a phone call home that Shirl had placed hours earlier in a nearby town. It had somehow had found its way to the portable phone that the native guide apparently carried for emergencies. Although there were no known power stations in the area to relay the phone signal, we guessed that the freak electrical storm had somehow completed the connection.

Now, if we can be standing at a sacred site on the upper edge of the earth, fully anticipating a world-altering message from the Ancient Ones, and receive a cellular phone call in an environment where one cannot possibly occur, we can certainly access the inner truth that is waiting for us in our in-basket.

Reality is determined by the one perceiving it.

All we have to do is *believe*.

chapter 24

The Impossible Just Takes Longer

BY BEING RECEPTIVE to the variety of possibilities that the universe has to offer, you can begin to avail yourself of the virtually unlimited range of opportunities available for personal and spiritual growth. It's basically the same concept that Norman Vincent Peale introduced to us in his best seller, *The Power of Positive Thinking* (Prentice Hall, 1987). It's what your mom told you when you were a little putter who was a bit short on self-confidence. It's what shamans have been demonstrating for centuries.

The key word here is *intention*. For example, if you were to visit a locker room before an important football game and listen to the coach expounding on his belief that there was no way his players could win the game, you would probably agree that the coach's approach falls a bit short of creating a winning consciousness. Believing that the team can't possibly succeed only reinforces the likelihood that the losing point of view will become reality.

We don't need to consult a Rhodes scholar to deduce that the same conditions apply to the tenets of parapsychology. Once you begin to eliminate doubts and negative thinking from your conscious mind, you begin to unlock the door to your creative self.

If you can accept the concept that you create your own reality, consider this: your spirit guides provide you with what you request. *I guess you want limitations,* your guides might assume, if you're one who tends to dwell on negativity. *Why else would you constantly affirm a limited point of view?*

Affirmations are like prayers. When we pray, we release the thoughts (prayers) we wish fulfilled. Why, then, should we be surprised when the negative thoughts and limitations that we allow ourselves to believe are manifested? After all, everything is created or manifested by us out of energy—and since our thoughts are energy, our thoughts create form. Our spirit guides are only delivering what we've requested.

Why Science Can't Explain God

People who don't believe in paranormal events often perceive things in terms of logical or scientific measurement. For example, scientists in the field of mainstream physics, chemistry, biology, and the neurosciences view reality and matter in terms of physical substance, energy forces, and particles. They conclude that consciousness is entirely explainable as an emergent epiphenomenon. That means it results from, but has *no* reciprocal effect or subsequent influence on, the material realm.

On the other hand, spiritually-based thinkers believe that everything is part of a universal consciousness field—an aspect of the Creator Force. They contend that this all-inclusive field is God expressing Itself through thought. What God thinks *is*. If we are truly created in God's image, then what *we* think, we too can create. It's a simple matter of energy.

Reality without Limitation

Ever notice how we tend to deny an experience if we cannot rationalize or understand it? We may not be able to explain the cause of a religious experience or medical miracle—but does that mean that it hasn't occurred? Stars and planets occasionally behave in opposition to long-accepted laws of physics. Should we negate the existence of unfathomable forces based on the fact that we have never physically seen them?

Certainly, we can't discount something as impossible just because we've never witnessed it. The construction of the massive pyramids and the creation of numerous mysterious images on Easter Island would be problematic under that model.

So would the phenomenon of someone who possesses the ability to walk though a solid block wall, eighteen inches thick.

There have been reports that human skeletons have been found in the outer bulwark of antediluvian Tibetan monasteries. Since these walls consisted entirely of solid rock fragments bound together by minimal amounts of mortar, one is forced to conclude that the original owner of the skeleton had to have been trapped in the masonry *after* the structure was constructed. Obviously, the bodies could not have been placed in the wall during construction, since the structure was devoid of hollow spaces or voided areas to account for the presence of flesh.

Legends suggest that ancient sects of monks had mastered many of the mysteries of the universe, including the ability to penetrate solid objects. Is it possible that those men learned how to rearrange the molecular structure of their bodies in such a way that they were able to pierce the solid surfaces of dense stone? Perhaps the ones whose bones were found in the walls lost their concentration during their initiation ceremony and became eternally trapped in the granite and mortar.

Many believe that the ancient Egyptians possessed esoteric knowledge as well. Consider the precise construction of the temples and pyramids, their methods of embalming the dead, their detailed knowledge of the solar system and creation of the calendar. As was true in many ancient cultures, a neophyte entering their secret societies had to prove his or her mastery of this knowledge before being accepted as a member. For example, it is written that apprentices of the mystery schools were required to negotiate an underwater passageway below the temple of Kom Ombo along the Nile River. To accomplish this, they were required to hold their breath in the dark passage with alligators lurking about, relying on only their subtle knowledge and intuitive skills to survive the trial.

To fail was to die.

Later, when allowed into the Great Pyramid, they were commanded to journey through the lower passageways in order to confront the physical manifestations of their greatest fears. Many books, such as *Initiation* by Elisabeth Haich (Seed Center, 1965) and *Initiation in the Great Pyramid* by Earlyne Chaney (Astara, 1987), suggest that these ancient Egyptians relied solely on their metaphysical skills to lead them to the initiation site in the King's Chamber. Many authors go so far as to claim that they were required to travel out-of-body in order to pass through the solid masonry block ceiling and enter the secret chamber located directly above.

Could these stories possibly be true? Well, the fact that the Great Pyramid was constructed on the *exact* geographic center of the land mass of the earth certainly suggests that it possessed a special significance. The fact that the height of the Pyramid corresponds to the average height of the earth above sea level seems more than coincidental. And that's not all. If you divide the perimeter by twice the height you get 3.1428 . . ., the value of *pi*—a basic mathematical formula that to our knowledge was first discovered by Archimedes in 250 B.C.E. Historians say that the Great Pyramid was built no later than 2,500 B.C.E.—and many metaphysicians (myself included) believe it was built as many as ten centuries earlier[1] than that. Its four sides face the cardinal points of the compass, verifiable by instruments known only for the last two centuries. In fact, Peter Tompkins' book, *Secrets of the Great Pyramid* (Harper & Row, 1971), suggests that it is a scale model of the hemisphere, correctly incorporating the geographical degrees of latitude and longitude.

A mere burial place for a pharaoh? I think not.

There are those who accept the historical existence of the continent of Atlantis and the ability of its people to harness mysterious natural energy forces unknown to us today. The mystery schools and secret societies of the Middle Ages possessed similar mystical knowledge and kept it hidden from all those who might misuse it.

Stories of alchemists who had the power to transform lead into gold and who dispensed the elixir of perpetual youth abound through mythology. Gold was thought to be the one perfect (solar) metal. It was said to symbolize spirit, immortality, and spiritual freedom. Not only was it valuable as a source of wealth—mystics felt that it prolonged life when absorbed by the body. However, true immortality was said to be identical to enlightenment—the Eastern traditions believed that the cycle of birth and death involved only those who had not attained the knowledge of immortal truth.

Were these beliefs only fables? Fanciful fairy tales and wishful thinking? Joseph Campbell, a well-known chronicler of myths, has pointed out that legends, fairy tales, and mythology are almost always based on some aspect of historical truth.

---

1. According to Graham Hancock's *The Message of the Sphynx* (Random House, 1996), John Anthony West (a highly regarded Egyptologist), Dr. Robert Schoch (Professor of Geology at Boston University), and Thomas Dobecki (Chief Seismologist from the Houston firm of McBride-Ratclif & Associates) conducted geological and seismic surveys in and around the Pyramids at Giza. They concluded that the pattern of erosion on the Sphinx indicated that it was carved at the end of the last Ice Age, when heavy rains fell on the eastern Sahara—perhaps more than 14,000 years ago.

Could these stories be based on fact? Before you answer, consider the reaction that someone from a hundred years ago would have to telephones, fax machines, and television. Would they believe you if you told them that you have the ability to instantly communicate with someone on the other side of the planet merely by speaking into an instrument in your home? Or that you could insert a written document into a small desktop device and it would be reproduced and delivered to a remote recipient in mere moments? Or that we could—at the *push of a button*—still receive incessant *Gilligan's Island* reruns on a rectangular box located in the living room?

I wonder what that person might say about the following story, which I know to be just as true as the telephones, fax machines, and TV sets that we take for granted every day.

The **Impossible Truth**

A well-known and respected psychic colleague of mine (let's call him Jack) decided he needed to escape from his self-imposed, pressure-filled existence. After much deliberation, Jack resolved to take a year-long leave of absence from the corporate fast lane and escape to a monastery in the far-off mountains of Tibet. His goal was to search for an understanding of the true nature of reality—something he could not achieve while maintaining his lifestyle in the United States.

After living the cloistered life in peace and spiritual harmony for almost a year, he received word that his father had unexpectedly died. The funeral was being delayed several days as the family awaited Jack's arrival. The problem was that the only airline flight that would get him home on time was scheduled to depart just hours after he had been notified of his dad's passing. Unfortunately, the airport was a full day's journey from the mountaintop—there was no way he could get there in time to catch the plane.

After relaying all of this to his mentors, Jack was led to a garden and counseled to sit quietly. As he closed his eyes in meditation, he began to sort through old memories. The truth of the distressing news began to sink in. He realized that he would not be able to attend his father's funeral, but he began to visualize the experience of physically being there.

Soon he became aware that he had been joined on his bench by a monk. As he opened his eyes, he found himself drawn to the peaceful radiance of this new arrival, whom he had never seen before. After a few moments, the monk quietly asked Jack how he could help ease his grief. Jack replied that the only thing that could help was to somehow be on the plane headed home.

"Everything is possible," the monk said softly, his smiling face glowing with compassion.

Jack returned to his own thoughts. He felt surprisingly at ease, considering the news he had just received. As he sat there, he found himself drifting in the warm and peaceful currents of spiritual solitude. He could almost see himself joining his mom and family members at the grave site.

Losing all track of time, he suddenly felt like he needed to walk. He stood up and began to meander through the garden that he had grown to love during his all-too-brief stay. He felt his pace quicken. The euphoria of the peaceful energy made him slightly dizzy. Suddenly, there was a flash of light and he blacked out for what seemed to be a moment or two. As he paused and closed his eyes to regain his bearings, he became aware of confusing sounds slowly increasing in intensity around him.

Gathering himself together, he forced his eyes open to discover that he was walking though a crowd of people, all oblivious to him, each focused on his or her own thoughts. He heard an amplified voice on a public address system announce something about Los Angeles.

As he looked around, he realized that he was in a crowded airport, approaching an airline counter. He looked up at a pretty face smiling at him and asking, in an accent heavy with British overtones, if she could help. As he brought his hand forward to the counter to steady himself, she reached out and took something he was holding.

It was an airline ticket.

"Just in time," she said smiling. "You almost missed your flight. May I see your passport?"

"My passport?" he replied weakly.

"Yes," she said, "I think I see it in your breast pocket."

He followed the direction of her finger and withdrew the small blue book.

"Okay—thanks," she finished. "Go ahead through that door."

Mesmerized, he fell into line behind several other people moving in the same direction. *I must be dreaming*, he thought. *Where am I? How did I get here?*

He followed the woman ahead of him into the plane and turned toward the central cabin.

"Excuse me," said a voice wearing the uniform of a flight attendant. "Ahhh, excuse me sir, but you don't belong here."

"What?" he responded, knowing that this entire scenario was too good to be true. He blinked his eyes, expecting to wake from a dream.

"This is coach. You have a first class ticket, sir. Your seat is up there."

Not only was he at an airport he couldn't possibly have arrived at in time, on a flight bound for home for which he had not purchased a ticket—but he had a *first class seat!*

When this happens to you, you *gotta* believe.

chapter 25

Gettin' the Energy to Flow

MANY SKEPTICS WHO take the time to investigate paranormal occurrences with an open mind discover the reality of psychic phenomenon. However, there is often greater resistance in believing that we, *ourselves*, are psychic. You may concede that while others possess these extrasensory abilities, you have never had a true metaphysical experience.

Nothing could be further from the truth.

Have you ever approached a physical location and experienced a funny feeling? Perhaps, as you entered a room, you felt uncomfortable but could not ascertain the reason why? Maybe, as you set foot in a familiar environment, you sensed that something was wrong—but couldn't quite put your finger on it. Have you ever had to get out of bed in the middle of the night to make a pit stop and somehow known exactly what time it is? Or been able to wake up moments before the alarm goes off? Or answered the phone and discovered that the person you were just thinking of calling is on the line? Or known what someone was going to say moments before they actually spoke?

You have? And I thought you said you weren't psychic . . . .

The **Sixth Sense**

Being psychic is about feeling or *sensing* the energy of things—discerning the subliminal vibrations of a person or object on a subconscious level. Each of us does this all the time without giving it much thought. We often *know* things but assume that we must have read about it somewhere or, perhaps, have somehow figured it out logically—we rarely give credit to our intuitive or psychic nature.

The central control mechanism for this natural means of perception is your sixth chakra, located on your forehead just above the bridge of your nose. Remember the old movies where Cleopatra wears a headband in the shape of a cobra curled upward across her forehead? Historically, this metal strip was worn to protect the third eye—the chakra center that perceives psychic images. Ever notice how someone will absentmindedly place their finger on their forehead when pondering a thought? Whether they are conscious of it or not, they are activating their psychic sight, working to visualize an answer to the problem at hand.

Not only can we sense psychic energy with our third eye, but we can see it with our physical eyes as well. An aura, in its broadest sense, is the energy field that surrounds each living thing. To see yours, situate yourself in front of a mirror in a semi-darkened room and stare at your third eye with "soft eyes." With your peripheral vision, begin to discern the white light outlining your head. The result will be similar to what you see when you gaze down a road in the summertime and notice a white, wavy heat band distorting objects in the distance.

With enough practice, you'll be able to differentiate specific colors in your aura. Begin this process by imagining what the colors might be if you could see them. Gradually, you will be able to perceive them outright—and it doesn't end there.

Not only do you have the ability to sense and *see* the energy . . . I'm here to tell you that most of the time, you can even *alter* it.

The Alteration of Energy

Can you recall ever entering a space where people have congregated and sensing collective anxiety among the assembled group? It is said that we can sometimes "cut the tension with a knife." This is because energy is modified by consensus—it is altered by a majority of the group of people experiencing it.

We can all relate to encountering a group of people having a good time and being uplifted by their enthusiasm. Attend a football game and you will likely become part of the group energy of the crowd. When everyone begins doing the "wave," you feel the energy move through the stadium. You can sense that the momentum of the game changes when one team is inspired by a series of successful plays.

Sports fans are familiar with the concept of home-field advantage. Spectators can actually alter the outcome of the game by intensifying and directing their collective energy in support of their team. When the locals have fallen behind in a game and the organist begins to play that tiresome "Dum, dum, dum, dum . . .," you can feel the energy of the crowd heighten. The fans begin to clap, yell, and converge their collective intention on their sports heroes. When this occurs, anyone who has played the game will tell you that the home team physically receives a measurable lift. You can learn to do the same thing in your daily life.

Once you become adept at sensing energy, you can alter it by focusing on whatever it is that you wish to accomplish.

What do we need to know to be able to do this?

The Science of Manifestation

Manifesting your desires is something of a science. We could elaborate on the molecular-level electron bonding relationships of energy and the solid-state bioelectromagnetic field's interaction with the electromagnetic activity of matter—but let's keep it simple. All we really need to have a handle on is a very basic principle.

Quantum physics suggests that we are each expressions of an infinite and universal field of energy. In other words, we are part of the "all that is," and the *all* in "all that is" is *energy*. Deepak Chopra, author of *Quantum Healing* (Bantam Books, 1989) and *Ageless Body, Timeless Mind* (Random House, 1997) states:

> *All of us are connected to patterns of intelligence that govern the whole cosmos. Our bodies are part of a universal body, our minds an aspect of a universal mind.*[1]

Chopra suggests that we are beings of energy and that our bodies reflect the focus and expression of this energy. As we redirect energy, we can alter form. Furthermore, our *thoughts* are energy that, when focused properly, can eventually affect or manifest physical being.

In a similar vein, Dr. Andrew Weil, in his book *Spontaneous Healing* (Knopf, 1995), writes:

> *The more you experience yourself as energy, the easier it is not to identify yourself with your physical body.*[2]

1. Chopra, Deepak. *Quantum Healing: Exploring the Frontiers of Mind/Body Medicine* (New York: Bantam Books, 1989).

2. Weil, M.D., Andrew. *Spontaneous Healing: How to Discover and Enhance Your Body's Natural Ability to Maintain and Heal Itself* (New York: Knopf, 1995).

Weil implies that if you associate yourself more with your spiritual energy—and less with your physical torso and emotional limitations—you will be much more successful at manifesting whatever it is that you want or need.

Getting What You Want

There are, of course, many methods to get what we want. There are several self-help books and workshop techniques out there that suggest we should focus on altering energy rather than playing power games in order to manifest our desires.

What does this mean?

Well, let's say that you have requested assistance from a salesperson or friend and you find that you're getting less than you expected. You are continually requesting specific action but find that the person you're dealing with is consistently giving you the runaround— your needs are not being met.

Instead of informing this person that *you* are right and *he* is wrong, this technique encourages you to remain in your power . . . *your* control. You might respond to each balking statement: "Yes, I understand that—but I don't have what I need."

After several such exchanges, the person might become defensive and deny responsibility for your problem, suggesting instead that you are at fault. "Maybe you didn't understand—," or "I never agreed to that!" he might retort.

Your response is always the same: "Yes, that's possible . . . but I don't have what I need."

Each time he assumes the offensive or fortifies his position, you simply *restate your need*. Even if he becomes accusatory and snaps at you with something like "Can't you see I'm busy?" or "I don't know what you expected . . ." you merely quietly restate your desire—focus on your objective, manifest your goal.

Generally, this is the point in time when many a belly will tighten and veins begin to bulge in anticipation of a confrontation. Each participant typically digs in, intent on firming their position, resolved to prove the other party *wrong*.

And guess what? In that scenario, at least one side loses.

The key to success with this method is to stay focused on what you want—that way, you won't have to waste effort engaging in a confrontation trying to make the other guy wrong. As a result, you will eventually gain your objective.

All you need do is to calmly continue to reiterate your position, thereby manifesting the desired result. In the case of the salesperson or friend, who knows? If the situation is handled properly, they might even decide to help you. The point is, you will have achieved your goal—*your* truth—without denying the other guy theirs.

Let go of winning and you'll get what you want.

Visualize Success

We can psychically manifest what we want by holding on to the image of our success, becoming attached to the desired results before they happen. This procedure is not unlike an athlete who pictures himself clearing the high jump bar or an individual who seeks the perfect mate. It is simply the practice of programming the desired results.

A key to the success of this process, however, is to become attached to the *emotion*, not the form, that you wish to create. A person wishing to manifest a permanent relationship, for instance, should focus more on the emotion that is desired than on the physical characteristics of the new partner. Be more concerned about how you *feel* and less about what he or she will look like. Since being psychic is about feelings, you will achieve greater success if you concentrate on what you wish to *feel*.

Seeking a relationship is primarily about seeking love, companionship, and security. These are emotions. If we concentrate our efforts on creating a handsome or beautiful mate, we may not get what we truly desire. Let the universe provide the form—if you think about it, the universe has many more options than you do.

Intention and Attention

We can influence the outcome of *any* situation with our intention. We can even recall and learn from our dreams if we state our intention to do so by placing a pad of paper and pencil next to our bed before retiring. The moment we awake, we maintain the *intention* to recall the emotions and images we encountered while dreaming.

The important companion to intention is *attention*. We are often presented with information from our guides or psychic self in the form of a feeling—but we frequently write it off as an inapplicable notion. Learn to recognize that your feelings are meaningful.

If you experience a positive sense about something, then stay with it—literally perceive it inside your physical body and absorb it into your awareness. Associate with the sensation as though you are remembering a conscious event that has already taken place.

If, on the other hand, you experience an undesirable emotion, consider it a warning and *manifest an acceptable alternative.* Imagine that you are cleaning out the refrigerator as you do this—you know that discarding the sour milk is important, but don't forget that you must replace it with something else, or you won't have anything to drink. We often are so intent on avoiding what we *don't* want that we forget to replace it with what we desire.

The Means to Support Your Intentions

If you feel comfortable working with tangible objects, empower a religious symbol, quartz crystal, boji stone, or precious heirloom from a family member to assist you in altering energy. This can be done by focusing your intent on the object, defining its task, and believing that it can fulfill the purpose you have given it. Tai Ch'i masters, Tibetan sages, and modern shamans routinely use highly charged crystals or rocks from a sacred site to cleanse and alter a client's aura during the treatment of an illness.

Remember, Dorothy returned home from Oz only *after* she believed in the magic of the ruby slippers.

You can also use your chosen tool to enhance or magnify your intention to establish protection. Remember our discussion about manifesting a circle of light around you in order to protect your body? Why not use the same concept to protect your house, neighborhood or family members when they are at some distance? The spiritual light can be sourced from your inner essence, of course—or you can draw it from a favorite crystal, a family Bible, or a physical aspect of nature, as we have already discussed.

Shirl and I won't get on an airplane until we have encased it in spiritual light. I recall channeling the same idea to a client during a reading, instructing her to mentally extend the protective spiritual God light out from her house to the freeway and along the route she takes each day to and from the office. She found that she had begun to experience stress as she approached her home after a hard day's work, anticipating her teenage children.

Following her guides' specific instructions, she discovered that she not only found the house to be more peaceful upon her arrival, but she could more easily make the adjustment from working woman to understanding parent. The commute to her home now became something like a time warp, providing her safe passage in which to complete her change of identity.

Another example: When I was on my vision quest in the Sierras, my fear of being alone was my greatest concern. I found that I could protect myself by periodically walking in a large circle around my campsite and visualizing a light barrier—a ring of fire—protecting me. When I retired for the night, I would visually charge the circle with loving energy from my inner light. The intention of this exercise was to prevent any of the multitudes of scary unknown physical or mental monsters from coming to get me.

It worked! Not only did I enjoy a safe camping experience, but the fear that I had anticipated all but dissipated.

Of course, you can never guarantee that things or events will automatically or magically change to meet your assumed needs. There is a greater power in the universe, and It has It's own agenda— to say nothing of the needs of the people around you.

Keep in mind that some obstacles are, in fact, gifts—opportunities that are continuously provided so that you might resolve your own personal karma. Even so, don't give up on doing something to alter your energy. Doing nothing will negate *any* influence you inherently possess regarding potential opportunities that may be coming your way.

chapter 26

The Exception to the Rule

Now that you have gained some insight relating to the modification of psychic energy, you need to be aware of a small disclaimer. There are always exceptions to the rules, aren't there? I before E, except after C—and there's always a cop around, except when you really need one.

The same rule applies to manifestation: you can always change the energy . . . *except* when you don't believe that you can.

According to many ancient traditions, manifesting what you desire is a relatively simple procedure. It has been mastered by shamans from a variety of worldwide cultures. It was practiced by the powerful ancient Egyptians at the height of their domination of the civilized world. It has been known by mystical sages, avatars, and seers throughout recorded history.

Manifestation was a well-kept secret by the powerful mystery schools known to have existed throughout Europe for thousands of years. They described it as a three-step process, so simple that it has been disregarded by most people who have discovered it in the ancient texts. The method might be best presented in the context of the following story.

The Gypsy Village

While Shirl and I were in Brazil with Dr. Stanley Krippner, one of the world's foremost authorities on shamanistic practice, we were provided an opportunity to test the manifestation method during a visit to an exotic community known as Valley of the Dawn.

Valley of the Dawn is a remote and self-sufficient commune, acknowledged for their unusual and colorful healing rituals and elaborate initiation ceremonies. It was frequented by both the hardcore followers of an esoteric alternative healing sect as well as the spiritually curious from all over the world. We had apparently just missed seeing Shirley MacLaine, who had been there to gather information for one of her books.

Following infrequent and misleading road signs along narrow, bumpy, and unpaved roads, our van arrived at the outskirts of the village at midday. It was a shanty-town settlement of several hundred residents with the ambience of a carnival.

Upon exiting the vehicle, Dr. Krippner gathered us together and suggested that we prepare ourselves for a unique event. Shirl and I closed our eyes and immediately began to center and ground ourselves, as was our practice when confronting unknown situations.

"You may never see anything quite like this," said Dr. Krippner.

Talk about an understatement!

The hamlet had all the earmarks of a gypsy encampment: narrow dirt lanes lined with poorly constructed open air shelters assembled from what might kindly be referred to as substandard surplus materials. All of the paths led to the central plaza and the healing center, which consisted primarily of a tall imposing structure constructed of discarded metal siding. It looked like the movie set of a large, abandoned Air Force Quonset hut constructed for an old World War II motion picture. I almost expected to see John Wayne come swaggering out of the large structure, dressed in vintage battle gear.

Behind the huge central building was a large concrete pool, massive enough to accommodate an Olympic swim meet. We were informed by one of the local citizenry that it was a ritual site used for initiation ceremonies. She added nonchalantly that these ceremonies included periodic visits from friendly intergalactic space travelers.

We didn't meet anyone claiming to possess the registration to an alien spacecraft, but after observing the residents one could believe that almost anything was possible . . . .

We were directed to the entrance of the auditorium-sized healing center where we received a brief and unemotional indoctrination delivered by a woman whose selection of clothing was, shall we say, colorfully uncoordinated.

As our guide explained the procedures we were about to observe, I realized that numerous healings would be occurring simultaneously. My main concern in light of this fact was being in the proximity of an intense concentration of discarded negative energy. It seemed a lot like deciding to enter a crowded room where everyone has the flu and is casually spitting their germs out into the open. The chance of being infected would be rather high.

Another major concern was the fact that *like attracts like*. As strange as it might sound, I was worried that additional, external, negative forces might be drawn to this place.

When our guide finished her discourse, she motioned for us to follow her into the healing temple proper. Shirl and I debated about entering the building but soon relented to the pressure of the majority and the fact we had traveled a great distance to see this curiosity. As we were led through a maze of dimly lit rooms and nonaligned passageways, Shirl and I both noticed that the further we ventured into the building, the more dizzy and disoriented we became.

Our eyes quickly grew accustomed to the darkness and we observed numerous healers, mostly working in pairs. One would perform the healing ritual while the second assisted, steadying or holding the patient. This process, known as "magnetic passes," is said to remove the negative energies (or discarnate spirits) that have attached themselves to the physical body and are causing the discomfort or illness. Many spiritual healers believe that if the negative energy is left in place, the host body can ultimately be possessed by this foreign energy force.

The primary healer would begin by rapidly shaking both of his hands in the air as if to energize or magnetize them. After locating an area of discomfort, the practitioner would place his hands on or slightly above the aberrant energy field. With a quick motion, he or she would draw them downward, as though repelling water off their body and onto the floor. During the entire process, the healer would shout in Portuguese—apparently commanding the invisible spirit to leave—while the patient often would wail or moan, seemingly in torment.

As you can imagine, there was an overwhelming sense of disorganization and confusion in the temple. Loud disharmonious sounds could be heard emanating from the forty or fifty rituals simultaneously taking place. The entire procedure seemed highly unusual to Shirl and me, having observed ritual healings throughout the world conducted generally with a greater dignity and reverence.

Typically, the healing work that we've observed has been performed by a single practitioner, although there are many instances when others are asked to assist in the removal or disposal of the discarded energy. Often these helpers are asked to maintain the energy of the space while chanting or drumming.

In Valley of the Dawn, no attempt was made to neutralize the negative energy once it was removed. This is equivalent to leaving infectious diseased tissue on the floor after surgery, ready to infect all who come into its proximity.

As we proceeded toward an area of particularly intense activity, Shirl suddenly stopped and closed her eyes.

"I'm so sleepy . . ." she said slowly as her knees began to wobble. "I think I have to lie down for a moment."

Oh my God, I thought. *Dorothy had the same experience in the poppy field on the way to the Emerald City!* I looked around, somehow expecting to see the green-faced Wicked Witch of the East rubbing her hands together in glee.

Where were the Munchkins when we needed them?

I grabbed Shirley by the shoulders and gently shook her.

"What . . . ?" she stammered, as if being rudely wakened from an unscheduled mid-day nap.

"Are you okay?" I asked, attempting to break the strange and sudden spell that appeared to be steadily enveloping my life-partner.

"I don't know. I just feel so *tired*."

I sat her down on a nearby bench while my eyes instinctively searched for a side exit, which I knew probably did not exist. I felt powerless as I witnessed her helplessly submit to this unknown negative energy force. The highly charged and confused intensity from the people around us was mixed with the discarded negative energy from multiple healings—it was sapping her strength. I immediately instructed Shirl to ground herself and stay within her power as I attempted to help her resist this increasing oppression.

After a moment she seemed to snap out of it and stood up, assuring me that she was okay and wanted to continue on our tour. However, we had no sooner begun to move forward to rejoin our group when Shirl did it again. Her knees buckled and she fell like a limp doll to the floor.

I held onto her arm and, with the help of another member of our traveling party, reversed direction to search for a doorway leading outside. Disregarding the shrill voice of our resident tour leader who was insisting that we must all stay together, we moved toward the exit, stopping every ten steps or so to prop up the sagging body of my wife.

After what seemed like an endless time warp, we located the front entrance and our means of escape. It felt like we were physically pulled into the clean, refreshing texture of the open environment—repelled from the heavy force of the negative energy like a magnet laid end to end with another in a high school physics class. Shirl seemed to feel it, too. She began to walk under her own power as we neared daylight.

Once outside the enclosure, she quickly recovered and began to return to her old self within minutes.

The **Three-Step** ## Method **of Manifestation**

The fact that the abundance of negative energy left lying about affected those of us in the tour group who were particularly sensitive is not surprising. In like form, a professional musician will squirm at badly performed music and a fashion designer will feel uncomfortable with a disturbing meld of colors and fabrics. In fact, negative energy can often be *so* highly repugnant that it seems to have a greater charge than if it were a positive force of equal intensity.

A key point of note is that the more fearful we became about the effects of excessive negative energy in the temple, the more power and intensity it generated. We know that fear is not *always* a bad thing—*when we can benefit from it*. On a *CNN* interview some time back, Michael Eisner, the Disney CEO, was asked the secret of his success—what motivates him? His one-word, honest, straight to the point answer was:

"Fear!"

However, as we discussed in chapter 21, when we allow fear to gain power over us to the degree that it begins to dominate our thinking, we can no longer benefit from it. Ancient wisdom and shamanic teachings remind us that to compensate for this unyielding and oppressive fear, we need only manifest what we want.

This brings us back to the three-step method for successful manifestation that is outlined in the hidden libraries of secret societies. The steps are simple:

1. *Know what you want.*

   In the case of the healing temple, Shirl needed to remove herself from the negative energy and its harmful influences and align herself with the positive energy of the open air and the natural healing qualities of the earth.

2. *Know that you have it.*

   Shirl and I both pictured health and freedom, visualizing ourselves in positive energy, separated from the suffocating negative influences that were affecting our bodies. Consequently, we were led to the entrance despite the confusing labyrinth of passageways hindering our progress.

3. *Let go (of your fear or limitation).*

   As we released the overwhelming fear that gripped and held us in its power, we began to make room for the result we so desperately desired.

Once in the open air, Shirl found a group of young children and began to speak to them. Seemingly both parties were unconcerned about the fact that neither spoke the other's language. She joined in the children's games and laughter, and soon found herself in the simple and pure energy that she needed to completely rejuvenate.

She was able to escape from what did not serve her *only* when she identified and manifested what she required.

I'm reminded of the old joke about the man who went to the doctor and lifted his arm over his head.

chapter 27

Making a New Beginning

OKAY—GET OUT your pencils and paper and put away your notes. It's time to determine whether or not you've been paying attention. This will *not* be a pop quiz like the ones sprung on you in high school. There will be no letter grades given and no instructors to impress. The results won't be posted in a public place for all the world to see.

It will, however, have a direct bearing on whether you graduate to the next level of understanding.

Think of this test as a homework assignment through which you will be provided the opportunity to showcase your newly discovered knowledge in an area with which you are familiar . . . you see, this test is called *real life*.

Now that you're finishing with this book, you've opened a doorway to a new adventure—like it or not. There's no going back to the way things were. You have everything you need to get started.

How you act upon it is entirely up to you.

Some of you who have already discovered your spiritual path to enlightenment will have recognized what you read in the previous pages as truth. This may have been a wonderful means of reviewing what you already know—or simply a pleasant reminder of what you may have forgotten along the way.

Others of you who are a bit more cautious may have found the material to be interesting—food for thought. You may have concluded that *some* of these concepts *might* be possible and at least worth investigating. You may have decided to proceed slowly on a slightly new path while carefully exploring these new alternatives.

Still others may have consciously chosen to disregard the whole thing as baloney, labeling most of it as logically impossible and assuming that the text is either an exercise designed to puff up the author's ego or an opportunity for him to make another few cents each time one of these little puppies is sold.

Regardless of your conclusions or reactions, there is no avoiding the fact that you *have* been changed.

What I sincerely hope you take from these pages is that it's all about a new beginning—a new way of *being*. It's about knowing that your reality is nothing more or less than your perception of it. For example—name a vegetable that you love. I may inform you that the very same vegetable is on *my* endangered species list. Can both of us be speaking the truth? Is it possible that my truth is different than yours? Of course!

What I have attempted to impart to you, my dear reader, is the that you design your own truth. Your truth is uniquely yours—known only to you and experienced only by you. I, of course, have my own truth, as does the person next to you and the guy driving the bus. We each perceive things differently. We each have our own truth. What you may not have realized until now is that *we possess the ability to change it.*

This material was intended to demonstrate that we are each psychic . . . or intuitive . . . or aware—all of these words express the same concept. Each of us inherently possesses the ability to access our higher knowing for the purpose of spiritual growth and understanding. Each of us was issued the necessary operational equipment at birth.

Some of us need only to turn it on.

Inform your guides tonight, before you venture off to wherever the sleep elves carry you, that you are ready—ready to discover a whole new way of being. Ready to discover your truth. Dump the old tapes, jettison the old ways, eliminate the limited thinking. Not unlike the religious belief that our sins will be forgiven when we repent, you can believe that you will expand into your true being when you readjust your way of thinking. It's easy—just do it!

Whether you have felt that the concepts presented here are valid or invalid (possibly approaching the outer limits of the twilight zone), know that this book has just touched the surface. There is much more out there to learn and explore about the true nature of spiritual and physical existence. Much of it can't be read in a book.

The thought I wish to leave you with is that everything in this universe is basically *energy*. Einstein proved that with his $E=MC^2$ thing. What we call *positive* energy has infinitely more power than negative energy. Love is the most powerful of those forces—it's the strongest energy in the universe. Love is, in fact, probably the word most often chosen to describe God. Why else would the Bible teach us to love our enemies? Love has a far greater authority than anger, fear, or despair. By creating what we want through loving thoughts, as we did when neutralizing the negative energy in the Brazilian healing temple, our limitations will begin to dissipate and lose their power.

There are many illustrations of the positive power of love. One of my favorite stories about it took place at our youngest child's wedding, for which I served as minister. After the bride had walked down the aisle, I discovered to my great dismay that the large candle the bride and groom were to light during the conclusion of the ceremony was already burning. The scripted plan was to have the mothers of the bride and groom ignite their candles from a small candle tucked away beneath the larger one, walk the flames to their individual children who, in turn, would then light the larger candle, signifying their joining together as one.

Unfortunately, the smaller source candle had not been lit—and the larger one was already ablaze.

What to do . . . ?

I caught the eye of Greg, my stepson and a member of the wedding party, who was in the proximity of the two candles. After discerning part of the problem from my series of head gestures and lip movements, he managed to subtly extinguish the flame on the larger candle, but failed to understand that the lower candle still required lighting.

I called on Amy, my more creative spirit guide, for assistance.

It was an outdoor wedding on a very hot day, and the festivities were being performed under the direct rays of the sun. *It's hot enough for the candle to light by itself,* I thought quietly, picturing the smaller candle with a flame, as it had been during rehearsal.

As we approached the time for the candle lighting ritual, I felt the hard stare of someone in the front row. It was Shirl, who was attempting to get my attention.

"Look at the candle . . ." her lips were saying.

The small candle had lit by itself.

Now, there are two possible explanations for what transpired. The first elucidation would suggest that the rays of the sun had passed through the protective glass cylinder around the larger candle and had somehow caused the spontaneous lighting of the smaller candle placed below it. I noticed that the glass encasement had been cracked and a piece had broken off. Perhaps the jagged edge of the broken surface had acted as a magnifying glass, refocusing the rays of the sun on the wick of the lower candle and thereby lighting it in the process.

The second option was to believe in the magic and love of the moment. Like I said—who cares what the postman looks like, as long as he delivers the check!

We have been thought into existence by, and in the form of, the Creator. This energy provides countless and continual opportunities for us to discover our own way of being and, in the process, to grow spiritually.

A female mystic from India who is said to have come to the full knowledge of the One, says:

> *Spiritual growth is a process of purifying our minds—*
> *stripping away the false ideas that keep us from our*
> *higher self.*

Stripping away the false ideas—the illusions—that limit us and prevent us from growing into our true being . . . and opening to your psychic potential is one means to enlightenment that is *continually* at your disposal.

It is my fondest wish that this book will inspire you to discover and use your natural metaphysical abilities . . . or, conceivably, motivate you to enhance the special aptitudes that are appropriate for your spiritual growth—aptitudes that are vastly more powerful and personal than you can imagine.

Whatever you do, *know* that you can do it. *Discover* your truth. *Create* your illusion.

And do it *your* way!

Namaste!

Bibliography

Benson, Herbert. *The Relaxation Response.* New York: Morrow, 1975.

Chaney, Earlyne. *Initiation in the Great Pyramid.* Upland, CA: Astara, 1987.

Chopra, Deepak. *Ageless Body, Timeless Mind: The Quantum Alternative to Growing Old.* New York: Random House, 1997.

———. *Quantum Healing: Exploring the Frontiers of Mind/Body Medicine.* New York: Bantam Books, 1989.

Coburn, Chuck. *Funny You Should Say That...: A Lighthearted Awakening to Psychic Awareness.* Redway, CA: Seed Center, 1995.

Graham, Billy. *Angels: God's Secret Agents.* Garden City, NY: Doubleday, 1975.

Haich, Elisabeth. *Initiation.* Palo Alto, CA: Seed Center, 1965.

Hancock, Graham. *The Message of the Sphynx.* New York: Random House, 1996.

Lemescuier, Peter. *The Great Pyramid Decoded.* Great Britain: Element Books, 1977.

Moody, Raymond and Paul Perry. *Reunions: Visionary Encounters with Departed Loved Ones.* New York: Villard Books, 1993.

Peale, Norman Vincent. *The Power of Positive Thinking*. New York: Prentice Hall Press, 1987.

Perkins, John. *Psychonavigation: Shamanic Techniques for Travel Beyond Time*. Rochester, VT: Destiny Books, 1990.

————. *Shapeshifting: Shamanic Techniques for Global Transformation*. Rochester, VT: Destiny Books, 1997.

————. *The World As You Dream It*. Rochester, VT: Destiny Books, 1994.

Redfield, James. *The Celestine Prophecy: An Adventure*. New York: Warner, 1993.

Roberts, Jane. *Seth Speaks: The Eternal Validity of the Soul*. Englewood Cliffs, NJ: Prentice Hall, 1972.

Smith, Penelope. *Animal Talk.* Point Reyes, CA: Pegasus Publications, 1989.

Tompkins, Peter. *Secrets of the Great Pyramid*. New York: Harper & Row, 1971.

Walsh, Neale Donald. Conversations with God. New York: G. P. Putnam's Sons, 1996.

Weil, M.D., Andrew. *Spontaneous Healing: How to Discover and Enhance Your Body's Natural Ability to Maintain and Heal Itself*. New York: Knopf, 1995.

Wesselman, Hank. *Spiritwalker: Messages from the Future*. New York: Bantam Books, 1995.

Index

A

Abraham, 53, 66, 193

affirmations, 33, 186-187, 200

Africa, 4, 42, 46, 54, 74, 160-162

alchemy, 76, 203

aliens, 4, 16-17, 24, 67, 118, 189-190, 197, 219

altered energy, 9, 41-42, 209-211, 213, 215

ancient societies, 202, 218

Andes, 14, 23, 31, 39, 46, 169

angels, 43, 52, 54, 65-68, 71, 73, 75, 78, 94, 97, 111, 116, 137, 149, 151-152, 205

animal psychic, 79-80

astral body, 32-33

astral projection (see also out-of-body), 32-33, 127, 153

astrology, 4, 82

Atlantis, 203

aura, 15, 33, 48, 137, 177, 189, 208-209, 213

ayahuasca, 10-14, 16-17, 21-22, 24, 27, 36, 41, 49, 62-63, 173, 182

B

Big Bang, 93

Buddha, 193

C

camaying, 14, 17, 39, 46-48

Campbell, Joseph, 203

Cayce, Edgar, 4

ceremony (see also ritual), 6, 10-11, 13-16, 22-23, 32-33, 44, 46, 48-49, 54, 56-58, 60, 74, 101, 106, 114, 116-118, 124, 126, 163, 173, 182, 184, 186-187, 202, 218-219, 228

chakra, 15, 19, 48, 105, 127-128, 155, 208

Chaney, Earlyne, 202

channeling, 15, 33, 44, 73-74, 76-79, 81, 91-92, 94, 123, 126, 128-129, 145, 147, 166-167, 214, 224

chanting, 18, 32-34, 46, 96, 102, 173, 186, 220

chincha, 10, 14, 27

Chopra, Deepak, 210

Christ, 4, 55, 77, 82, 193, 196

Christianity, 66-67, 126, 179

clairaudience, 40, 112

clairessence, 112

clairvoyance, 33, 40, 112, 141

closure (see also protection), 65, 86, 111, 113, 125-127, 129

coincidence, 71, 85, 88, 94, 144, 151, 156, 202

consciousness, 3-5, 7-8, 14, 18, 22, 24, 36, 41-44, 56, 68, 77-79, 94-95, 105, 115, 126-129, 131, 151-154, 164, 178, 188, 194, 200-201

Creator Force (see God)

Czar Alexander II, 53

D

Day of the Dead, 55-56

de Padua, Antonio, 15

death (see also transition), 8, 12-13, 15-16, 25, 28, 35, 37, 44, 48, 52-57, 60-61, 93, 97, 112, 114-115, 119, 123-124, 137, 152, 167, 172-173, 176, 184, 188, 193, 195, 202-205

Delphi, Oracle of, 60, 75

depossession, 42-43

Dia de Los Murtos, 55-56

discarnates (see ghosts), 127, 220

divination, 60, 81-82

dolphins, 79, 87-88, 90

dreams (see also psychic dreams), 2, 5, 7, 18, 49, 51, 58, 60, 68, 94, 113-114, 138, 152-157, 163-164, 166, 182, 188, 190, 194, 206, 213

E

Ecuador, 2-4, 6-7, 9-12, 14, 23, 31, 34, 39, 41, 43, 45-49, 58, 62, 74, 102, 105, 155, 162, 169-170, 182

Egypt, 19, 60, 184, 202-203, 218

Einstein, Albert, 9, 227

electrical disturbance, 120

emotions, 10, 15, 18, 23, 33, 42, 49, 56, 58, 60, 88, 107, 113, 124, 126-128, 131, 134-136, 141, 143-144, 152-153, 155, 159-160, 168, 173-174, 178, 181, 183, 186, 190, 194, 211-213

esoteric knowledge, 7, 95, 202

exorcism, 116

F

fear, 18, 22-23, 25, 27-29, 35-36, 48, 66, 75, 86, 98, 106, 115, 120, 124, 127-128, 141, 152, 162, 168, 173-174, 176-184, 187, 189-190, 214, 222-223, 227

forty, 55, 173, 203, 220

fragrances, 33, 115, 176

funeral, 53-54, 204-205

G

Gabriel, Juan, 23, 25-26, 34-36, 46

ghosts (see also discarnates), 2, 15, 42, 52-55, 58-59, 65, 75, 77, 111-121, 123-124, 171-173, 175-177, 184, 190

God, 40, 56, 65-67, 73, 92, 94, 98, 103-106, 118, 129, 137, 188, 200-201, 210, 214, 221, 227, 229

Goddess, 4, 9, 163
Graham, Billy, 67, 203
Great Pyramid, 202-203
Greece, 75
grounding, 103-106

H

Haich, Elisabeth, 202
Halloween, 54-56, 60-61
healing, 2-4, 9-11, 13-18, 22-23, 31-
    35, 37, 39-42, 44-49, 56-58, 67,
    74, 76-77, 79-80, 104-105, 114,
    135, 151, 160, 162, 186, 189,
    210, 218-221, 223, 227
Heaven, 2, 66, 179, 183, 193
Heck, Jim, 1, 57, 161
Hell, 179
higher self (see also third self), 107-
    108, 130, 229
Hoerig, Diane, 77

I

I Ching, 74, 76, 82
imaginary friends, 149, 151
intention, 9, 83, 86, 97-99, 105-107,
    111-112, 114, 117, 160, 188, 199,
    209, 213-214

J

Joan of Arc, 66
karma, 3, 29, 34, 92-93, 97, 107,
    112, 129, 137, 145, 154, 179,
    182-183, 192, 195, 215

K

Knight, J. Z., 77
Krippner, Stanley, 67, 218
Kundalini, 18-19, 36

L

Lemuria, 77
Lincoln, Abraham, 53
lower world, 43, 171, 179
lucid dreams, 153-154

M

MacLaine, Shirley, 77, 218
magic, 43, 70-71, 76, 102, 141, 183,
    214-215, 229
magnetic passes, 220
male energy (see also yang), 4
manifestation, 10, 53, 66, 68, 74,
    86, 95, 97-98, 108, 112, 142, 145,
    151, 189, 193, 196, 200, 202,
    210-214, 217-218, 222-223
manteum, 59-63, 65, 97, 172, 175,
    177, 179, 182
Masons, 76
Massai, 160
medicine man, 14
medicine wheel, 103, 187-189
meditation, 5, 41, 45, 83-84, 94-96,
    98-99, 103, 123, 126, 146-147,
    204
messages (see psychic messages)
middle world, 43
missionaries, 8, 169-170

Mother Earth (see also Pachamama, Nunqui), 10, 22, 74

mystery schools, 202-203, 218

N

Napoleon III, 53

Native Americans, 14, 48, 58, 74, 103-104, 117, 185-188

negative energy, 39-42, 48, 57, 97, 104, 106, 115-116, 118, 122, 125, 127, 219-223, 227

negative thought, 43, 130, 167, 200

Newton, Sir Isaac, 8, 86

Noetic science, 2

Nunkqui (see also Pachamama, Mother Earth), 9

O

obsession, 3, 42, 115

occult, 76, 171

oracles, 3, 60, 75

orashas, 74

Otavalo medicine man, 14

out-of-body, 14, 63, 68, 127, 153, 202

P

Pachamama (see also Nunqui, Mother Earth), 10, 33, 46, 104

Pai Ely, 56-58, 112

palmistry, 76, 81-82

paranormal, 2-3, 51, 167, 174, 200, 207

past lives (see also reincarnation), 54, 80, 92-93, 97, 107, 167-168

Perkins, John, 7-8, 13, 17, 49

personal growth, 2, 10, 78, 82, 84, 86, 97-98, 113, 155, 182, 188, 191, 199, 226-227, 229

planetary consciousness, 4, 7, 102, 169

positive energy, 223, 227

possession, 41-42, 115

power animal, 14, 43, 78

prayer, 41, 44-45, 186, 188, 200

Prince Albert, 53

protection (see also closure), 104-105, 111, 118, 126, 214

psychic channel (see channeling)

psychic dreams (see also lucid dreams), 152, 156-157

psychic messages, 18, 47, 56, 60, 66, 76, 78-80, 82-83, 98, 114, 118-119, 123, 129-130, 150, 159, 187, 197, 203

psychic surgery, 15, 41, 56

psychics, 3-4, 23, 33, 41, 47, 75-77, 79, 87, 91, 95, 115, 141, 144-145, 166, 173, 177, 188, 203, 229

psychonavigation, 49

pyramid, 201-203

Q

quantum physics, 9, 95, 210

Quechua, 10, 31, 33

Queen Victoria, 53

R

rain forest, 2, 7-8, 10, 12, 14, 21-24, 28-29, 36, 41, 47, 62, 102, 105, 169, 173, 182

reality, 3-5, 8-9, 15, 17-18, 28, 40, 43, 62-64, 78, 88, 96, 103, 108, 112, 114, 127, 132, 139, 145, 147, 150-155, 159, 170, 177, 179, 181, 184, 187-188, 192-194, 196, 198, 200-201, 204, 207, 226

reincarnation, 92

ritual (see also ceremony), 12, 33, 58, 101, 103, 124, 186-188, 218-220, 228

Roberts, Jane, 78

Rosicrucians, 76

runes, 76, 82

Ryerson, Kevin, 77

S

sacred circle, 103

sacred knowledge, 8, 49, 76, 94, 166, 188, 223

sacred sites, 3, 102, 162, 197, 213

sacred space, 103

Samhain, 55

secret societies, 76, 202-203, 223

Serengeti Plain, 162

séance, 53, 76, 120

shamanism (see also healing), 1-5, 7-18, 22-24, 28, 31-37, 39-49, 52-53, 56-58, 60, 74, 77, 112, 125, 151, 155, 161-164, 178-179, 188, 199, 213, 217-218, 223

shapeshifting, 42

Shuar, 9, 11, 13, 26, 43

skepticism, 45, 121, 139-141, 165, 167, 183, 207

soul retrieval, 14, 41-42

sounds, 13, 22, 34, 37, 40, 52, 60, 71, 95-96, 106-107, 112, 118, 122-123, 131, 134-136, 147, 151-153, 156, 164, 166, 168-169, 176, 205, 220

Sphynx, 203

spirit guides, 3, 41, 43, 54, 58, 73-75, 78, 89, 91, 94-95, 97-98, 101, 106-108, 111, 113, 116, 126, 129, 131, 133, 142, 144, 147, 151, 189, 200, 228

spiritual path, 226

spiritualism, 44, 53, 76, 177

subtle body, 32, 127

sweat lodge, 6, 48, 186

synchronicity, 52, 56, 60, 71, 74, 82, 85-88, 90, 94, 99, 144, 176

T

Tai Ch'i, 213

tarot, 74, 76, 82-83, 86

telepathy, 47, 79-80, 129-130

third eye, 106, 127, 130, 208

third self, 18

Tompkins, Peter, 203

trago, 14, 16-17, 39, 46-47

transformation, 5, 32-33, 42, 48, 168, 189

transition, 4, 113, 115, 184

transmutation, 41-42

Tyburn Village, 120

U

UFO, 4, 16-17, 24, 67, 118, 189-190, 197, 219

V

Valley of the Dawn, 218, 221

vision quest, 6, 36, 184-187, 214

W

Weil, Andrew, 210-211

Y

yang, 15, 105

yin, 15, 105, 189

☾ REACH FOR THE MOON

Llewellyn publishes hundreds of books on your favorite subjects! To get these exciting books, including the ones on the following pages, check your local bookstore or order them directly from Llewellyn.

ORDER BY PHONE
- Call toll-free within the U.S. and Canada, 1-800-THE MOON
- In Minnesota, call (651) 291-1970
- We accept VISA, MasterCard, and American Express

ORDER BY MAIL
- Send the full price of your order (MN residents add 7% sales tax) in U.S. funds, plus postage & handling to:

    Llewellyn Worldwide
    P.O. Box 64383, Dept. K155-4
    St. Paul, MN 55164–0383, U.S.A.

POSTAGE & HANDLING
(For the U.S., Canada, and Mexico)
- $4.00 for orders $15.00 and under
- $5.00 for orders over $15.00
- No charge for orders over $100.00

We ship UPS in the continental United States. We ship standard mail to P.O. boxes. Orders shipped to Alaska, Hawaii, The Virgin Islands, and Puerto Rico are sent first-class mail. Orders shipped to Canada and Mexico are sent surface mail.

International orders: Airmail—add freight equal to price of each book to the total price of order, plus $5.00 for each non-book item (audio tapes, etc.).

Surface mail—Add $1.00 per item.

Allow 2 weeks for delivery on all orders.
Postage and handling rates subject to change.

DISCOUNTS
We offer a 20% discount to group leaders or agents. You must order a minimum of 5 copies of the same book to get our special quantity price.

FREE CATALOG

Get a free copy of our color catalog, *New Worlds of Mind and Spirit*. Subscribe for just $10.00 in the United States and Canada ($30.00 overseas, airmail). Many bookstores carry *New Worlds*—ask for it!

Visit our web site at www.llewellyn.com for more information.

Journey to
Machu Picchu

by Carol Cumes &
Rómulo Lizárraga Valencia

If you are drawn to the mystic beauty of the Andes, Machu Picchu and ancient Peruvian culture, Journey to Machu Picchu will connect you with the spiritual world of the Quechua—the native people of the Andes. Reading about the Andean world of inexplicable realities will draw you into the hearts of the gentle Quechua, whose primary goal is to live and work in harmony and balance with Mother Earth. Even if you cannot physically set your feet down on the grassy highlands of the Andes, this book will trigger your own journey of awakening as you begin to look inward to discover your own special purpose. Contains 62 color and more than 70 black and white photographs.

ISBN: 1-56718-186-4, 6 x 9, 264 pp., 32 pgs. color photos $19.95

To order, call 1-800-THE-MOON
Prices subject to change without notice

New Chakra Healing
by Cyndi Dale

This manual presents never-before-published information that makes a quantum leap in the current knowledge of the human energy centers, fields, and principles that govern the connection between the physical and spiritual realms. By working with your full energy body, you can heal all resistance to living a successful life. The traditional seven-chakra system was just the beginning of our understanding of the holistic human. Now Cyndi Dale's research uncovers a total of 32 energy centers: 12 physically oriented chakras, and 20 energy points that exist in the spiritual plane. She also discusses auras, rays, kundalini, mana energy, karma, dharma, and cords (energetic connections between people that serve as relationship contracts).

1-56718-200-3, 7 x 10, 304 pp., illus.   **$17.95**

Reincarnation

by Genevieve Lewis Paulson &
Stephen J. Paulson

Why is knowledge of your past lives of any value to your present life? Traumatic events from the past can create blocks to your current growth and joys. Attitudes can carry over that hold you back from healthy relationships. Irrational fears with no known cause can sometimes be traced back to events in previous lives.

Reincarnation shows you how to enter into your own meditative state and access your own experiences and knowledge. Explore your cycles of lives…soul mates and soul relationships…soul families and tribes…the akashic records…genetic influences…the many facets of karma and how to transmute it…the process of evolution…leading past life regressions for others…how to die gracefully…finding your soul teacher…opening to your intuition…and much more.

1-56718-511-8, 5 ³/₁₆ x 8, 224 pp., illus.   **$7.95**

Tarot for Beginners
by P. Scott Hollander

If you're just beginning a study of the Tarot, this book gives you a basic, straightforward definition of the meaning of each card that can be easily applied to any system of interpretation, with any Tarot deck, using any card layout. The main difference between this book and other books on the Tarot is that it's written in plain English—you need no prior knowledge of the Tarot or other arcane subjects to understand its mysteries, because this no-nonsense guide will make the symbolism of the Tarot completely accessible to you. You will receive an overview of of the cards of the Major and Minor Arcana in terms of their origin, purpose and interpretive uses as well as clear, in-depth descriptions and interpretations of each card.

1-56718-363-8, 5¼ x 8, 352 pp., illus.   **$12.95**

Shapeshifter Tarot Kit

*by D. J. Conway and
Sirona Knight*

illustrated by Lisa Hunt

Like the ancient Celts, you can now practice the shamanic art of shapeshifting and access the knowledge of the eagle, the oak tree or the ocean: wisdom that is inherently yours and resides within your very being. The Shapeshifter Tarot kit is your bridge between humans, animals and nature. The cards in this deck act as merging tools, allowing you to tap into the many different animal energies, together with the elemental qualities of air, fire, water and earth.

The accompanying book gives detailed explanations on how to use the cards, along with their full esoteric meanings, and mythological and magical roots. Exercises in shapeshifting, moving through gateways, doubling out, meditation and guided imagery give you the opportunity to enhance your levels of perception and awareness, allowing you to hone and accentuate your magical understanding and skill.

1-56718-384-0, Boxed kit: 81 full-color cards, book   **$29.95**

To order, call 1-800-THE-MOON
Prices subject to change without notice